TANKS

AN ILLUSTRATED HISTORY
OF FIGHTING VEHICLES

CREATED AND PRODUCED

BY

EDITA LAUSANNE

TANKS

AN ILLUSTRATED HISTORY OF FIGHTING VEHICLES

ARMIN HALLE

ILLUSTRATED BY CARLO DEMAND

CRESCENT BOOKS · NEW YORK

517115859

Copyright © MCMLXXI by Edita Lausanne

All rights reserved. No part of this publication may be reproduced, stored in a retrieval system, or transmitted, in any form or by any means, electronic, mechanical, photocopying, recording or otherwise without prior permission of the publishers.

This edition is published by Crescent Books a division of Crown Publishers, Inc. by arrangement with Edita Lausanne

a b c d e f g h

Printed in Spain

Depot Legal SE-317-1973
ISBN 84-399-1366-4

CONTENTS

PREFACE

Any present-day account of armored vehicles can already be described as retrospective, for the tank is a war machine without a future. To many people this statement may seem paradoxical. And yet it is obvious that the new defensive weapons render useless any technical improvement on tanks and the persisting existence of the classic tank troops. In contrast to the tumultuous evolution of the recent past, now it is no longer a question of weapon caliber, of projectile penetration force or thickness of armor. The exigencies of present techniques are far in advance of those that made possible the appearance of tanks on the battlefield at the beginning of the century.

The tank of the future would have to be a wonder-machine crammed with electronic equipment; it would cost millions to perfect, construct and maintain; only engineers would be able to look after it and use it... and this prodigy could be put out of action or completely destroyed with all its equipment by one projectile the price of which would be more than ridiculous in comparison. Certainly the tank of the future would be able to cross ditches and rivers, but first it would break down before the frightening disproportion between its cost and its military efficiency.

During the coming centuries the principles of twentieth-century tank construction will perhaps be modified to create machines capable of moving at the bottom of the sea or in extra-terrestrial space. And perhaps in the near future there will be experiments with destruction machines or with military vehicles made to hover on cushions of air or to fly by means of rotors.

The military armored vehicle has come to the end of its evolution and its history is now almost over. For many experts as for many specialized organizations the armored vehicle is already nothing more than a witness of recent wars and its history the subject of reflection. This book, then, can display and sum up almost the complete range and development of a fascinating and terrifying weapon.

The authors would like to take this opportunity to thank all the people and institutions that have helped them bring together the documents and illustrations used to create this work.

ARMIN HALLE   CARLO DEMAND

Antiquity

Jericho fell on the third day. On Wednesday, June 7, 1967, Colonel Ben-Ari, the commander of the First Israeli Armored Brigade in the Israeli-Arab War, reported the capture of the city by two battalions of his unit, which was made up of reservists. He had, as he remarked later, "enough trumpets" for the decisive battle. At nightfall, in the face of strenuous defense from the Jordan troops, his tanks had entered the city with all guns firing and smothered enemy opposition. Next morning he held Jericho firmly in his hands.

What a difference between this bald statement and the story a military correspondent sent from the front a few days later recalling an Old Testament text! According to Joshua, Jericho was the first city in the Canaanite-occupied Jordan valley to be attacked and captured by the Israelites. That happened over three thousand years ago, the journalist said, but what made today so different from that far distant past was the presence of the tanks in the city streets. No one who had driven through the venerable ruins in a British Centurion tank and read the fear in the eyes of the cowed Palestinian refugees in the nearby camp could help realizing that the inhabitants of twentieth-century Jericho must have had a far more harrowing experience than their ancestors of long ago.

It would be no easy matter to give him the lie. But as far as the terror sown by armored cars is concerned, there is reason to doubt that it was unknown to mankind before the machine age. The Bible itself says very clearly that already in Old Testament times war chariots that could boast many of the features of the modern tank achieved the same psychological effect. "And the Lord was with Juda, and he possessed the hill country: but was not able to destroy the inhabitants of the valley, because they had many chariots armed with scythes," we are told in the Book of Judges (i, 19). Besides informing us of the existence of these tank-like vehicles, the passage already points out the weapon's tactical advantages and drawbacks: the superiority of the chariot over infantry made it almost impossible for the latter to capture and occupy territory defended by chariots; on the other hand the hills in front of enemy territory could be occupied without risk because inaccessible to chariots, which were not very good at negotiating rough terrain.

It is hard to establish the exact date at which war chariots first appeared. Nor is it a matter of any great importance. Images on ancient vases and reliefs, finds made in graves and, later, written texts as well, warrant its attribution to the end of the fourth millennium before Christ. There is no doubt that the Sumerians, who were the most ancient inhabitants of Babylon, possessed heavy vehicles that could also be used in battle. They were as a rule extremely ponderous and clumsy, mounted on two or four disc wheels and pulled by draught animals. Owing to their great weight and to the use of asses, both wild and tame, they were obviously not very fast. And no historical evidence warrants the assumption that the war chariot of that far distant past was a decisive tactical weapon.

Consequently, the introduction of light, two-wheel chariots drawn by two fast, well-bred horses was a revolutionary innovation in the art of war. This improvement occurred in the first half of the second millennium B.C. It is attributed to the Aryans, who invaded Mesopotamia from Eurasia. There are many reasons to believe that the Aryans were responsible not only for the development but also for the dissemination of a weapon that had not previously been known to other peoples. They were adept at breeding and training horses, and their military victories over the Semitic states in Mesopotamia and Syria may well have been due to the superiority of their chariots.

Wherever the conquering Aryans appeared on the scene, war chariots were in use soon after. Fifteen hundred years before Christ that typically Asiatic weapon had penetrated

Chariots with four disc wheels drawn by asses used by the Babylonians.

the West as far as Egypt and its appearance in Mycenae means that it had already reached Europe. In the first century B.C. a peculiar type of war chariot appears in the far north. Historical documents tell us that the Celtic inhabitants of Ulster in the North of Ireland, who had come into contact with the Mycenaean civilization at an early date, invaded Connaught "with three strong, stout, battle-proof towers on wheels". Each of those towers was drawn by thirty Danish stallions.

These ponderous, tower-like vehicles were not designed for mobile warfare in the open field but for attacking the mighty walls that surrounded strongholds in ancient times. The earliest representations of these wheeled battering rams date from the days of the Assyrian king Ashurnasirpal. They were monstrous structures which could obviously be moved only a very short distance and that only in one direction. One of those pictured was mounted on six wheels. It was made of wood and its sides were protected

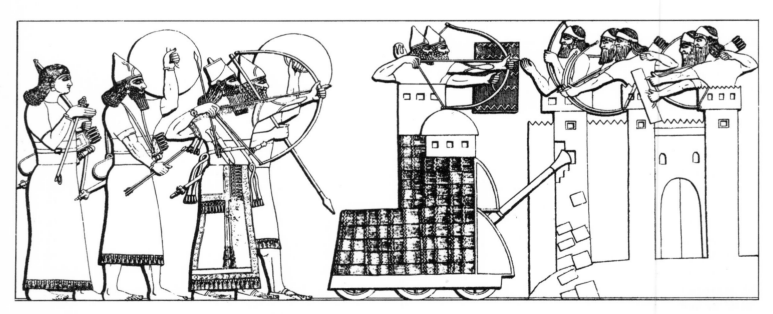

A heavy combat vehicle from the reign of Ashurnasirpal, King of Assyria (c. 870 B.C.).

10

Ramming power, protection and mobility were the major factors of the heavy Assyrian chariots, which were already used in mass formation in the ninth century B.C.

by tightly plaited wattles. It measured some twenty feet in length and ten in height. At the front rose a turret about ten feet high, which brought the total height of the front part to twenty feet. The turret was covered by a convex shield, probably of metal. Inside the turret the ramming beam, which projected from the front of the vehicle, was slung on a rope. This beam, whose tip was sharpened like the edge of an axe, could be set against a fortress wall at about fifteen feet above ground level and swung back and forth by the crew.

Most of the ram crew had no shelter, so archers were posted on other towers specially designed for that purpose to protect them from enemy fire. The wheeled towers manned only by archers were far taller than the twenty-foot ram turrets and correspondingly more ponderous. King Ashurnasirpal undoubtedly tried out many different types of wheeled battering rams. After him, his son Shalmaneser endeavoured to eliminate the greatest drawback of both rams and archery towers by having them built smaller and lighter. But already at that early date he must have had the same experience as the designers of

Lighter chariots were built under Shalmaneser III.

11

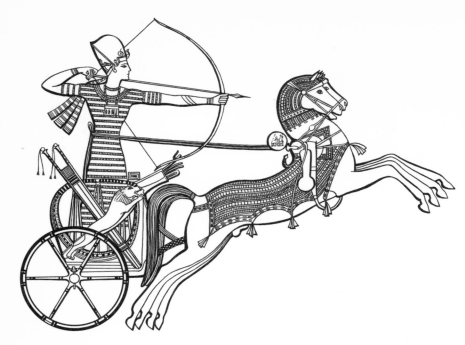

The noblest warriors were fond of being portrayed in a chariot: Ramses II at the Battle of Kadesh (1299 B.C.).

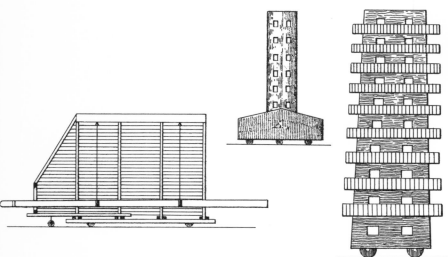

For attacking and laying siege to fortified positions the Greeks used mobile battering rams (bottom left) and combat towers up to a hundred feet high.

The scythe chariot—the Persian wonder weapon—did not fulfil the expectations designers and tactitians placed in it. This imaginary picture of a scythe chariot was in Vegetius' "Epitome Rei Militaris" in 1607.

modern tanks: namely that in combat vehicles greater mobility and cross-country capability can be obtained only at the cost of reducing their armor. In the case of the battering rams, it also involved reduced penetration.

But structural problems were not the only ones that the military commanders of that period had to tackle in connection with wheeled combat vehicles: there was also the problem of their correct tactical utilization. The introduction of the war chariot was followed by a boom in the weapons that corresponded to our firearms, namely bows and javelins. Nowadays it is imperative to equip tanks with guns that have the maximum rate of fire and range. In the same way ancient generals made every effort to outshoot the enemy chariot crews. They too did their best to employ their vehicles in close formation and throw as many as they possibly could into the fray. Thus at the Battle of Qarqar in 854 B.C. the Assyrian king Shalmaneser III faced some 65,000 men and about 4,000 chariots. The Egyptians, who had adopted war chariots at the same time as their foreign masters, the Hyksos, employed them in close formation with the same duties as mounted troops. The Persians, instead, started a battle by attacking simultaneously with their chariots and cavalry, leaving to the infantry the task of delivering the decisive blow.

The introduction of the war chariot led to an important innovation that had an essential impact on subsequent military history. Namely, the appearance of a class of fighters clearly distinguished from the rest of the army. This was undoubtedly the first germ of knighthood, which spread almost parallel to the war chariot in the area to the east of the Mediterranean and from there to Europe. It was closely linked with chariot fighting and horse breeding. Only the landed proprietors, members of a superior social class, could keep racing stables and give their horses all the care that they required. In addition, driving and fighting with a chariot demanded such intensive training that it took up all a man's time. It is interesting to note that the term employed throughout the Orient at that period to designate trained chariot fighters was *mariannu*—the Aryan word for knight. Ramses II too considered chariot fighters as the pick of his crack troops. Actually, in the Egyptian army war chariots were manned chiefly by foreign professional soldiers because the Egyptians themselves had not yet mastered the tactics of chariot warfare nor become familiar with wheeled battering rams and siege machines. Frobenius describes a chariot engagement in his *History of War on Land*: "It was the noblest warriors with the commanders in the van, who

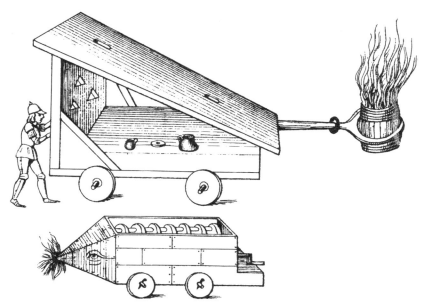

An Oriental fourteenth-century combat vehicle with "fire power". Vehicles that could spew or throw fire inflicted enormous damage on timber defenses.

A Roman war elephant with battle tower. The crossing of the Alps with elephants by the Carthaginian general Hannibal (247–183 B.C.) has become legendary. The great Mongol chief Kublai Khan still used war elephants at the end of the thirteenth century.

advanced at speed in their vehicles at the head of the attacking forces, to seek out their victims with spear and arrow in the enemy ranks and then withdraw no less swiftly. Two quivers full of arrows, a bent bow, a javelin and a battle axe were slung from the parapet of the two-wheel chariot, which was open towards the rear; the driver of the two or three horses stood beside the fighting man; in Asia a shield-bearer stood between the two."

The great respect in which chariot fighters were held in their day is demonstrated by the many reproductions of Assyrian and Egyptian potentates, who were pleased to have themselves portrayed standing erect in a fast-moving war chariot. In the case of the Egyptian kings, the driver was omitted in order to emphasize still further the dignity of the Pharaoh. Over two thousand years ago the Persians developed a special type of chariot that caused panic among the Greek mercenaries. It was the scythed chariot which was drawn by as many as eight horses and had sharp scythed blades attached to its wheel hubs and shaft; these blades revolved when the vehicle moved and must have ploughed huge furrows in the ranks of the enemy infantry. But the vehicles must also have broken the enemy cavalry and spoilt their impact. However, the Persian scythed chariots lost much of their value when foot soldiers learnt to open their ranks and let the unwieldy vehicles run through to no effect. At the Battle of Cunaxa in 401 B.C. between Cyrus and his brother Artaxerxes II, the former's Greek mercenaries routed the Persian scythed chariots when they stampeded the horses by shouting and

13

Siege operations in the Middle Ages: protected by screens and mantelets, miners attempt to breach the walls. Others fill in the moat so that the major assault weapon—the tower —can be brought into action.

beating their spears against their shields. Both chariots and cavalry fled before they could even shoot their arrows. This is how a Greek historian described the last phase of the battle: "The Greeks pursued them with all their forces but the scythed chariots, having lost their drivers, ran part through the hostile army, part through the Greeks. These latter opened their ranks, as planned; some of them were grazed, as happens on the racecourse, and dislodged from their positions but none were wounded."

Nonetheless, seventy years later—long after its tactical value had been put in doubt—the scythed chariot was still expected to be a telling weapon in the decisive battle of Gaugamela between Darius and Alexander the Great in 331 B.C. Darius had had broad areas of the battlefield in the plains of Nineveh levelled to provide a suitable terrain for his cavalry, particularly his scythed chariots. He felt certain of victory because he could count on Greek mercenaries, Persian horsemen, Indians on war elephants, and over two hundred scythed chariots. These he sent into the attack first in order to meet the heavy Macedonian cavalry under the most advantageous conditions. But the Macedonians, being drawn up in open formation, were able to evade the sharp blades. The chariots ran through them without doing any damage and were captured by the baggage train guards in the Macedonian rear.

No wonder the scythed chariot was used less and less as time went on, even though every effort was made to render the horses less vulnerable by changes in the design of the chariot. On only one other occasion did the scythed chariot win a victory by surprise: when used by a Bernese unit at the Battle of Laupen in 1339. Although the tactical trend seemingly made combat vehicles redundant, Roberto Valturio of Rimini, who was born in 1413, built one which he equipped with the very latest in long-range weapons: javelin, long-bow, cross-bow, matchlock and firebrand thrower. It too had scythes attached to the wheel hubs and was obviously inspired by ancient models. A good deal lighter and with lines that could almost be called elegant—if one can judge from the sketch—was a scythed chariot designed by Leonardo da Vinci in 1482. The blades were fitted not only on the hubs but also radially on a shaft at the front that was driven by one of the wheels. In addition to these two Italians, humanist scholars throughout Europe were impelled to design combat vehicles by their discovery of ancient battle histories. A work that must have been very stimulating in this respect was Caesar's *De Bello Gallico*, which not only describes infantry engagements but also gives a detailed account of the Britons' war chariots.

Combat vehicles of a novel type appeared during the Hussite wars in the fifteenth century. The transport wagons used for the purpose were steadily enlarged and

Technical drawing of a siege tower. The slight inclination towards the wall was designed to give the tower greater stability. A winch serves to lower the sally bridge onto the enemy fortifications.

The Incursion: the moat has been crossed; the tower stands before the wall and soldiers swarm up and across it in order to gain access to the town. The decisive phase of the operation is about to begin.

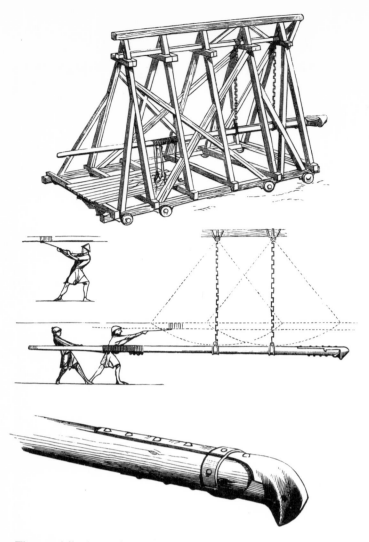

The mobile battering ram was often covered with timber or hide in order to protect the crew. The iron-tipped ramming beam suspended on long chains was swung in accordance with the laws of mechanics.

A wind-chariot with four-wheel drive. The vehicle shown here from the front and both sides was designed to be driven by the action of the wind on all four wheels through cog gears. It could only be used when the enemy position was down-wind. (After Roberto Valturio, c. 1475.)

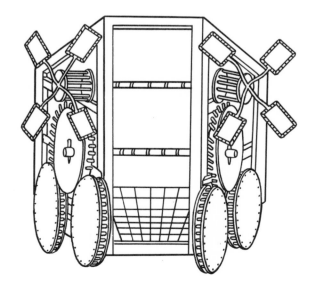

improved. They were finally reinforced at each side with timber walls behind which up to twenty men could take shelter—two for driving the team of horses, the others for fighting with weapons of different kinds. The tactical principles for their employment were still those described by Caesar in connection with the *esseda*, the combat vehicles used by Britons, Belgians and Gauls. First the wagon crew hurled missiles and shot arrows from aboard the vehicle; then they leapt out over the sides or back and continued to fight on foot. After the battle they mounted their wagons again. Like the tanks of the present day, these wagons gave support to the foot soldiers, who clustered around them in order to exploit the psychological impact on the enemy. The Hussite combat wagons carried implements—hatchets, shovels and pick-axes—which the crew used to clear the way over particularly rough terrain. They could also be fastened together, as had been done in the past by hordes of migrating peoples, to form easily defended laagers.

In 1456 the Scots invented a timber wagon that had room for the draught horses as well as the crew; but at the start the former had no protection and in consequence were very vulnerable. Later, the underpart of the wagon was timbered too, so that the horses were protected, but it made the vehicle very difficult to steer. The battle wagon reproduced in the war book written by a knight named Ludwig von Eyb was an improvement on the Scottish vehicle but may have been an original design based on ancient models. Though dated about 1500 it was mounted on thick disc wheels, which were almost completely obsolete at the time. On the other hand, von Eyb's sketch gives the idea of an almost modern profile with a ramming spur in front and loopholes at the sides. It also gives the first indication that combat vehicles were camouflaged with leaves and branches to conceal them from the enemy until the attack was launched. About 1558 Master Bertold Holzschuher of Nuremberg designed an assault car that bears an astonishing resemblance to the British "Willies" of World War I. But it displayed the same defects as its predecessors of Antiquity and the Middle Ages. The "armor" had necessarily to be strengthened in order to stand up to the increasing efficiency of throwing- and fire-arms; this made the vehicles more cumbersome. Ever since the introduction of combat vehicles, efforts had been made to combine the three factors armor, fire power and mobility to obtain the best results. Such clever inventors as Leonardo da Vinci, Ludwig von Eyb and Bertold Holzschuher may have guessed that a really practical combat vehicle could never exist so long as it depended on the horse for its motive power. In fact, the combat vehicle of modern times, namely the tank, was only developed when mechanical propulsion became feasible.

Two types of battering ram with artistically decorated heads. One of them, though designed 350 years before the first tank, is already shaped like a tortoise. (From Riuius' "Geometrische Buxmeisterei", Nuremberg 1547.)

17

The combat vehicle designed by Berthold Holzschuher of Nuremberg in 1558 had a very modern silhouette. Though it looks quite mobile it never left the drawing-board stage. It was to have been driven by horses attached inside or perhaps by manpower. However it was too heavy for combat.

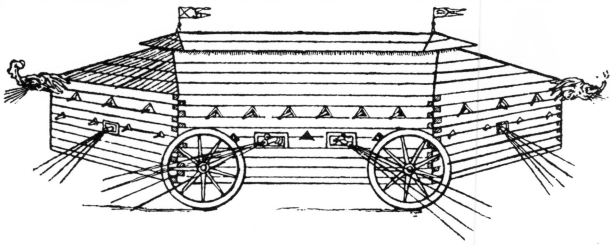

This drawing of a combat vehicle was printed in a book on artillery published in Nuremberg about 1470. The vehicle could move both forwards and backwards. The cannon was protected against infantry attack from below by an iron plate and a scythe. A wooden shield gave protection against arrows.

18

The Technological Age 2

If anyone were to call Leonardo da Vinci an "armament maker" and a "military theoretician" before a cultivated group of contemporary art lovers, he would certainly encounter massive, indignant criticism. But he would be quite right, nonetheless. First of all, he could point to the close connection between scientific research and military applications in Antiquity and the Middle Ages and take Leonardo's case as proof of how naturally the scholars, researchers and inventors of that time boasted of the advantages of their discoveries for military purposes.

"I shall also build safe, covered chariots that cannot be attacked, which, when they penetrate the enemy with their artillery, force even the greatest host of armed men to break. The infantry can follow in their wake with little risk and no resistance." In these words, written by Leonardo to Ludovico Sforza, Duke of Milan, in 1484, we find the germ of the tactics of mobile armored warfare. They anticipate the principles subsequently formulated in other terms for the use of tanks and tank troops which centuries later decided the outcome of two world wars.

Since all the cultivated men of that day, including writers and artists, followed with the greatest attention every advance in the natural sciences, the newly discovered laws of physics made an immediate impact in other fields. Albrecht Dürer busied himself with the study of military problems, first and foremost fortifications. When the Emperor Maximilian I made an alliance with King Henry VIII of England against the French in 1512, Dürer designed a number of combat vehicles for the Imperial army. He applied the law of the lever and invented various new systems of power transmission. Instead of being drawn by horses, his combat vehicles were driven by hand or foot power, and the crew used not only cranks and pedals but push rods too to move their cars. The Emperor, though very open to all new ideas, did not take Dürer's technical suggestions too seriously and so not

even a "prototype" was actually built. Only English horse-drawn cars were used at Guinegate and Flodden Field, where the French and their Scottish allies were defeated.

The next step towards a combat vehicle not drawn by horses was the "mobile bulwark" designed by the Nuremberg master craftsman Berthold Holzschuher, which not only possessed armor plating to protect the crew against enemy weapons and a device for hurling boiling oil and burning pitch, but was also equipped with the first known "four-wheel drive". Each wheel was manned by two stout men, who drove the massive vehicle by cranking them with all their might and main.

Holzschuher's design found many imitators. His fellow-citizen, the master craftsman Hans Hautsch, proved that good publicity served to make a new combat vehicle known and helped its inventor to achieve recognition and wealth. This is what was written about Hautsch's vehicle and his promotional ability: "However, a third citizen of Nuremberg, the clever wheelwright Hans Hautsch, won real fame in this field. In 1649 he amazed his fellow-

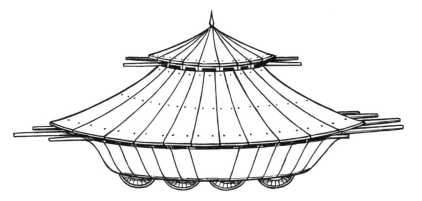

"I shall also build safe, covered chariots that cannot be attacked, which, when they penetrate the enemy with their artillery, force even the greatest host of armed men to break." (Leonardo da Vinci to Ludovico il Moro, 1484.)

Armored gun chariot with an officer at the command post. This vehicle, which was designed about 1500, was propelled forward by men pushing from the inside. (From "Epitome Rei Militaris" by Flavius Vegetius Renatus.)

townsmen with a 'Triumphal Car' that ran over the bumpy roads as if driven by a ghost. Master Hautsch sat proudly at the tiller, that was clear to see. But what one did not see was the lusty fellows who crouched inside the body of the vehicle and strenuously turned the driving crank. Hautsch also incorporated a very special invention in this unique car. It was the first vehicle with a signalling system: and what a drastic one it was. A dragon's head set firmly on the bow spewed water on any inquisitive spectators who blocked the road and so cleared the way for the driver."

It would not be too far-fetched to say that combat vehicle construction was in the doldrums. In fact it is not until over a century later that we find the description of an overland vehicle that displayed all the features of an

assault gun while still relying on men's muscles for driving power. "The two men standing in front are the master gunners who load and fire the gun. The man seated behind them is the aimer who steers the vehicle with the help of ropes connected with the rotatably-mounted front axle, and so aims the gun at the chosen target. The fourth and last crewman has the task of setting the whole vehicle in motion by turning a crank that acts on the rear axle through a cog-wheel gear."

Given such an unsatisfactory driving system, it is no wonder that every effort was made to find other ways of moving machines whose weight was increasing steadily. The amphibious vehicle invented by the Italian Agostino Ramelli in 1588 was drawn by a horse on land and propelled by hand-driven paddle wheels on water. But even this innovation could not eliminate the major drawback

Assault vehicle, sixteenth century.

Vehicles of this type were moved partly by horses attached inside, but their weight made them very unwieldy. The discrepancy between volume and available power was already being felt.

of all such combat vehicles, namely the discrepancy between the weight and volume of the vehicle and the human or animal power available. Even the sail, which had long been used to advantage at sea, proved useless when it came to propelling vehicles on land. A structural sketch dating from 1600 shows a wagon that was identical with contemporary sailing vessels right down to the smallest detail. But there is no evidence that it ever saw action.

Another landship that was designed to utilize wind power and also the latest technical advances was the wind power car. It had no sail but in its place windmill vanes at each side, whose rotary motion was transmitted to all four wheels by a cogwheel gear. Several specimens of this vehicle were actually built and employed on various occasions. But their scope was limited by the fact that they could only travel over dry, flat ground and only when

The idea of an amphibious combat vehicle that could navigate deep water thanks to two helical wheels dates from the sixteenth century. But even in the water this vehicle would have been too heavy for the manpower drive its inventor expected to use.

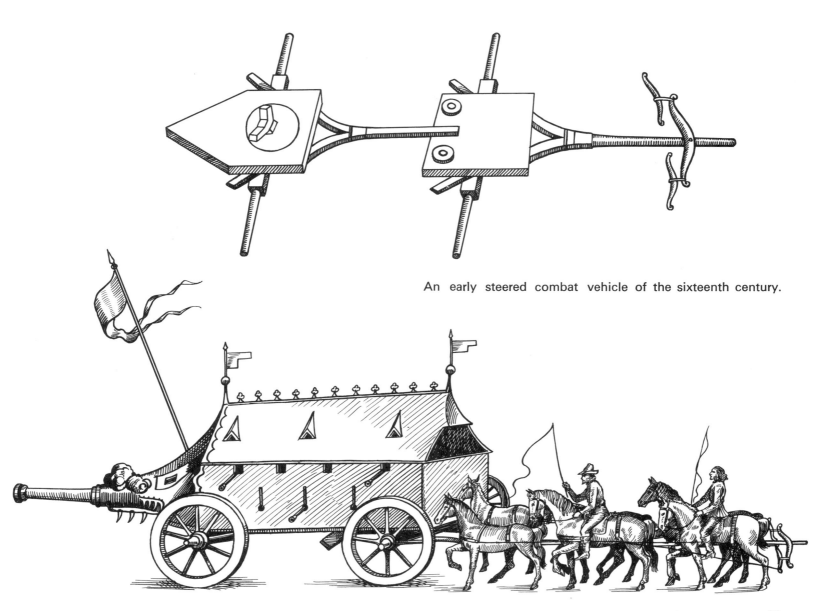

An early steered combat vehicle of the sixteenth century.

21

the wind was blowing towards the enemy—upon which a tactitian could not always count. Nonetheless a certain number of landships are recorded in documents at the beginning of the modern era. In 1599 Simon Stevin built a vehicle of this type for Prince Maurice of Nassau. It had a crew of 29 and a speed of 7 miles an hour with a favorable wind. In England a certain David Ramsay was granted a patent in 1634 for a self-propelled wagon that was also designed for military use.

After all these disappointing experiments a turning point seems to have been reached at last in the mid-eighteenth century, with the discovery of a new source of power constituted by the combined use of two elements that had long been known—fire and water. In 1765 James Watt succeeded in putting steam to practical use, and that marked a new stage in the development of military science. Four years later, in 1769, the Frenchman Joseph Cugnot set a steam engine on a wheeled chassis, which

Combat vehicle design in the doldrums: this eighteenth-century chariot had all the features of an "assault gun" but it would still have relied on human muscles for its driving power. The man stationed closest to the driving crank would have needed superhuman strength.

Even the steam engine—the new source of power—did little to promote the development of the combat vehicle. The power produced by the engine was consumed by its own weight and that of the fuel. The vehicle, armed with scythes, that was built by James Cowen in 1855 was virtually immobile.

thus became self-propelling. The next year he demonstrated the machine to the French ambassador to the Austrian court. But its maximum speed was only about 2 ½ miles an hour and it had to stop for a quarter of an hour every 12–15 minutes to build up pressure. Today we are inclined to think that to have got a machine to move at all by artificial means at that period in history was a considerable achievement, but people then were less long-sighted and Cugnot's demonstration was considered a failure. When Bonaparte, as a famous general, was elected to the French Academy he wrote a treatise on the military utilization of steam-driven combat vehicles, thus demonstrating his foresight in the domain of weaponry and armor.

In England too the discovery of the new source of power spurred inventors and designers to further efforts. In 1852, under the heading "Smith's Mobile Battery", the *Leipziger Illustrierte Zeitung* described the first combat vehicle that could offer protection against artillery, which was already highly developed at that time. "It is a small battery of one gun designed to move on ordinary roads. The plan, which was brought out by a certain Mr Smith of Drosford,

England, involves building it of iron sufficiently thick to resist the shots of the artillery that accompanies normal armies on the march. It forms a dome measuring 24 feet in length, 16 in breadth and 12 in height. These proportions, it is claimed, will allow the battery to move without difficulty up and down highways, which under English law must be at least 30 feet wide. In addition, the battery should, according to plan, be propelled by a steam engine that closely resembles 'Bray's Traction Engine'."

Smith was well aware of the drawbacks of his mobile fortress. This is proved by his idea of fitting directly under the front axle a massive cylinder equal in length to the entire width of the machine, whose weight it would support if the wheels happened to encounter soft ground. The armament of Smith's battery comprised 12 breech-loaders and a pivoting gun that could turn through 360 degrees and fire in any direction. What new strategic and tactical problems the design of a vehicle raised is shown by the following sentence in the German newspaper's description: "The Englishman thinks he is in a position to build a battery whose weight, including crew, armament and ammunition, is not in excess of that which normal bridges and roads can carry."

Steam was far more successful as motive power for ships and railway stock. So much so that only a few years after the steam engine started out on its triumphal march the first ironclad fighting ships appeared on the high seas and the first armored trains on the battlefields. We find armored trains during the American Civil War; accompanying the advance of the white settlers on the American continent; at the siege of Paris in 1871; in the Boer War and the Sudan campaign. They were composed of engines and wagons protected with heavy armor plates and equipped with cannon and machine guns.

The first steam-powered land vehicle not railbound that was ever employed in war was a three-wheeler. The boiler was suspended between the two rear wheels and the single, larger front wheel. The cannon was mounted on one side. This armored vehicle had no steering gear and could only move in one direction. It was used shortly before the French Revolution.

In the long run even the invention of the steam engine did not result in any real progress in the armored-vehicle field. Owing to the enormous weight of the ironclad monsters the friction between wheels and ground consumed a large fraction of the available power. But bigger and therefore more powerful engines required larger quantities of "fuel", namely coal and water, so that the actual useful load remained extremely low. The vital problem was to reduce the ratio of engine power to vehicle weight: it is still one of the toughest problems in tank construction.

It was not long, however, before new technological advances occurred. In 1876, over a century after Joseph Cugnot's efforts, Nikolaus Otto presented the first four-stroke compression engine, and Carl Benz built his first automobile in 1885. That would have never sufficed to bring about the actual breakthrough in armored-vehicle construction were it not for the appearance of another revolutionary factor at about the same time. Namely, the development of what a Germany military paper

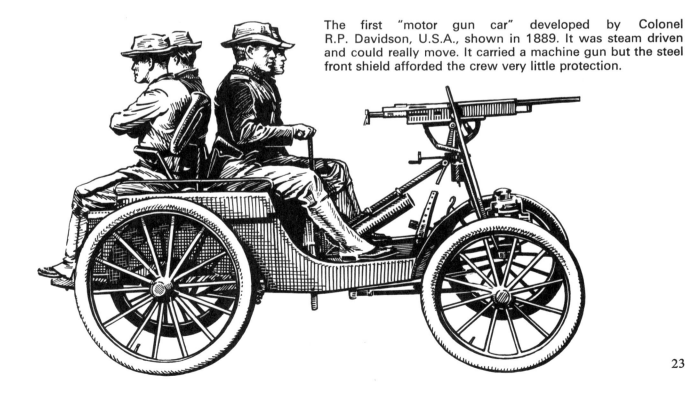

The first "motor gun car" developed by Colonel R.P. Davidson, U.S.A., shown in 1889. It was steam driven and could really move. It carried a machine gun but the steel front shield afforded the crew very little protection.

written in 1880 termed an "absolutely novel transport system by means of an endless iron track". The internal combustion engine and the caterpillar track are still the major structural features of the tank that shaped the image of two world wars and offers newly discovered advantages in the nuclear age.

The first mention of a caterpillar track dates back to the year 1825, when it seems to have been invented by a German named Krauterer. The mid-nineteenth century saw the appearance of steam tractors, which had lateral booms equipped with "feet and wheels" in order to spread

The imagination of the English combat vehicle designer Pennington was obviously too far in advance of the technological potential of his day. He drafted various plans and sketches for armored vehicles, some of which look quite modern. Here is one designed about 1902.

over a larger surface the enormous pressure they exerted on the ground and so reduce its specific value. They were employed during the Crimean War of 1854/55. But it was only in the Franco-Prussian War of 1870 that the military establishment realized the necessity of giving artillery and other heavy equipment cross-country capability by fitting them with a suitable undercarriage.

Julius Schneider, a German sapper born in Silesia in 1840, who gave much thought to this matter, wrote an essay entitled "On the Construction of Transport Wagons with Toothed Wheels on an Endless Tread", which was published in the *Archive for Artillery and Engineer Officers of the German Imperial Army* in 1872. He himself built small-scale demonstration models and wrote an explanatory note entitled "Track without End". Schneider was balked in his request for permission to dedicate this paper to the Emperor, who was his Commander-in-Chief. The embittered young captain recorded in his diary: "Doubts about the design of the car have been expressed on many sides and it has been described by high-ranking superior officers as not worth a practical trial. The idea was not even considered suitable for a memorandum."

As a matter of fact, Schneider succeeded later in having a chain-track car built. It made a good show in a trial run over the engineer corps training ground at Cologne, and in 1873 was put through severe, top-secret tests "under very unfavourable ground conditions" in Berlin. However, the Artillery Research Branch, who considered the captain a crank, took a poor view of his machine. After much quarrelling and friction with his superiors, not to mention an

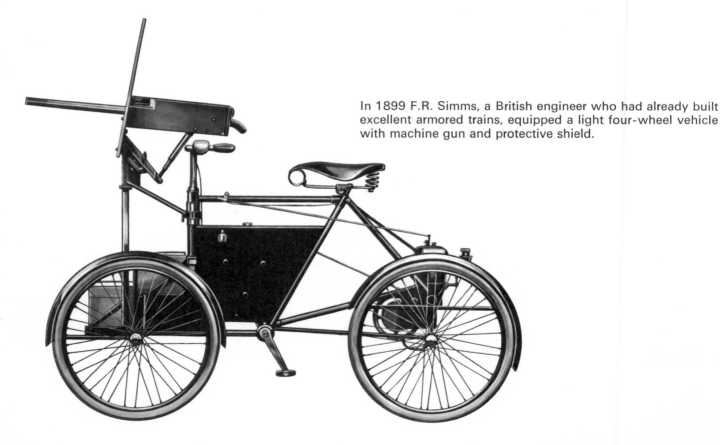

In 1899 F.R. Simms, a British engineer who had already built excellent armored trains, equipped a light four-wheel vehicle with machine gun and protective shield.

The first heavy armored car fitted with steel plating was developed by Simms in 1902 and built by Vickers. It looked like a ship on wheels. The "war motor car", as it was called, was designed for offensive and defensive operations. But, in spite of his earlier success with the railed tank, Simms did not succeed in selling it to the British army.

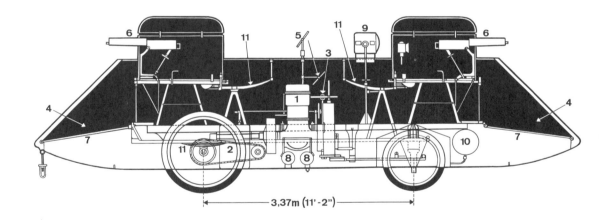

3,37m (11'-2")

1, engine;
2, gearbox;
3, steering wheel;
4, magazine;
5, mirror;
6, machine guns or cannon;
7, spring-loaded braces;
8, exhaust silencers;
9, searchlight;
10, fuel tank;
11, spring suspension;
12, light dynamo;
13, water tank;
14, driver's seat.

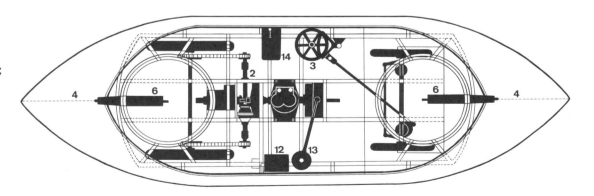

The Austro-Daimler armored car built in 1903–5 incorporated the major principles of those in use today: four-wheel drive, revolving turret with cannon or machine gun, and a crew composed of several specialists.

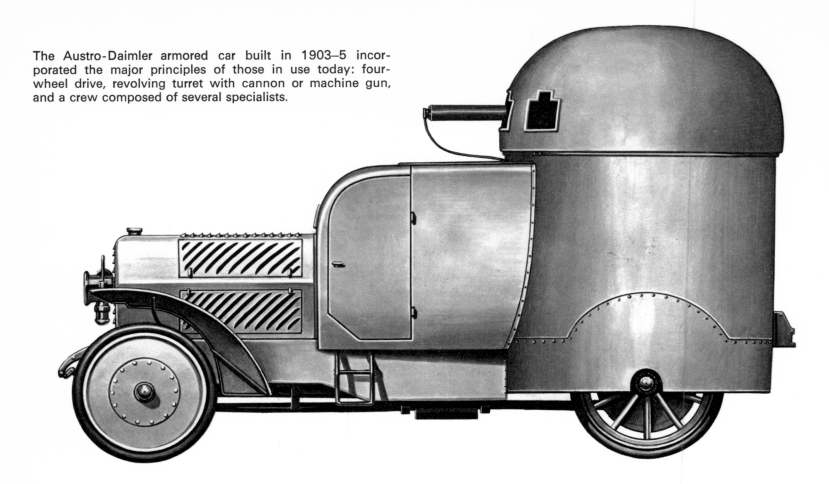

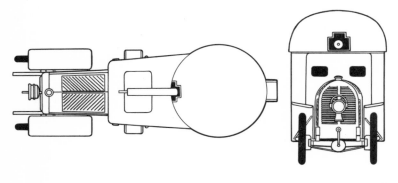

Armored Car, Austro-Daimler (Austria)

Weight	3.24 short tons, 2.9 long tons (2.95 tons)
Length	13 ft. 5 ¼ in. (4.1 m)
Width	7 ft. 2 ½ in. (2.1 m)
Height	8 ft. 10 ¼ in. (2.7 m)
Engine	Daimler, 4-cylinder, watercooled, 4.4 l, 30–35 h.p., 1050 r.p.m.
Speed	14–28 m.p.h. (24–45 km.p.h.)
Armament . . .	1 mg, later 2 mg
Armor	3 mm, turret 4 mm
Number in series .	one only
Year	1903–5
Price	27,000 Austrian krone

accident in service, Schneider resigned from the army. There followed repeated unsuccessful attempts to find useful applications of his invention in civilian life. In 1910 Schneider died at Kassel, where one of his demonstration models is preserved in the local museum.

The first motorized combat vehicles were developed simultaneously with these first trials with the "endless track" as the caterpillar track was then called. At the start, however, the design of armored cars for combat and reconnaissance was based on the four-wheel automobile. A long time passed before both paths converged and the motorized military vehicle was combined with the caterpillar-track chassis.

The first armed motor vehicle was designed by Colonel R.P. Davidson of the Illinois National Guard, who was a lecturer at the North-Western Military Academy. In 1889 he entrusted the task of building it to Charles E. Duryea, who had already built a petrol-engined passenger car. This first "motor gun car" was a three-wheeler armed with a machine gun and protected in front by a steel shield. It carried four men including the driver. Subsequently, the same design was adapted to a four-wheel chassis. Shortly after this the Academy commissioned two steam-

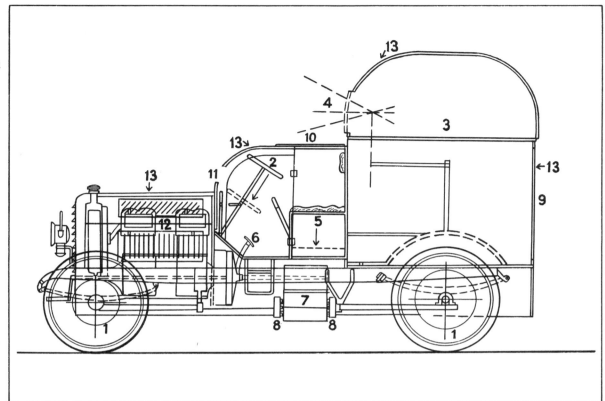

1, four-wheel drive;
2, pull-out steering wheel;
3, turret revolving through 360 degrees;
4, machine gun;
5, driver's drop seat;
6, accelerator;
7, gear-box;
8, brake;
9, turret hatch;
10, hatch;
11, hatch;
12, 30 h.p. Austro-Daimler four-stroke 4-cylinder carburettor engine;
13, 4-mm steel armor plating.

The Austro-Daimler of 1903–5 blazed the trail followed by other armored car designers throughout the world.

powered four-wheel combat cars that were also equipped with a machine gun and light armor plating. This enabled the cadets to obtain experience in the first motorized unit in the history of war. But the importance of the new weapon was far from being recognized at the time.

During that same period in England a man called Pennington was attracting a great deal of publicity to himself and his invention. In November 1896 he presented plans for a four-wheel armored car with two machine guns, which he had allegedly been commissioned to build by a British syndicate. The international press seems to have taken Pennington's announcements more seriously than he did himself. It is true, however, that he made the public on both sides of the English Channel conscious of the potentialities of the armored car. Moreover, his plans displayed a number of features that look extremely modern. For instance, the wheels were mounted under the armor, the sides of the car were smooth and canted to make missiles glance off more easily and the car presented the "tortoise silhouette" still typical of the modern tank.

In 1899 F.R. Simms, a British engineer, presented a Maxim gun mounted behind a steel shield on a four-wheel chassis. He gives the impression of having been far more serious than Pennington but met with less success. The "Motor Scout", as he called his machine, was driven by a number of people but the military would have nothing to do with it. The same is true of a 6-ton vehicle with boatshaped armor plating designed by Simms and built by a British firm in 1902. By that time, however, the armored car was so much talked of at the international level that competition between the Great Powers ensured its technical development.

In the very year that Simms attempted in vain to have his 6-ton vehicle adopted by the British armed forces, development started on the Continent on a vehicle that not long after was presented as the first fully armored overland reconnaissance car. From 1903 to 1905 the Daimler Motor Company at Wiener Neustadt realized their own plans, which subsequently proved to be the real breakthrough in armored car design. They embodied the principles of the modern armored reconnaissance car—four-wheel drive, revolving turret fitted with machine gun or light cannon and drop-seats for commander and gunners, who were thus able to avoid enemy fire by ducking down behind the armor plating. The vehicle, which weighed only two tons, was powered by a 30 h.p. Austro-Daimler four-cylinder four-stroke carburettor engine. It could withstand shrapnel and rifle fire up to a distance of about 350 yards. Thus it satisfied one of the demands of modern tanks: the enemy infantry were within range of its guns before they could attack it effectively. Although four-wheel drive was already known, it constituted the real technical novelty of the car. In 1905 Austro-Daimler patented their four-wheel drive, which was the final solution of two technical problems. First, the guide wheels were driven without the insertion of joints, which are very much subject to failure; secondly, the greatest power was applied direct to the working wheels so that all the other parts of the transmission could be kept weaker and therefore substantially lighter. The cupola of the armored turret could be rotated by a handcrank through 360 degrees, enabling the commander to concentrate on his task, whether combat or observation, independently of the direction in which the vehicle was travelling. This armored reconnaissance car held a crew of four or five and also had room for the necessary ammunition. Its top speed on a straight road was under 30 miles an hour.

When the Daimler armored car was employed in the Austrian Imperial manoeuvres of 1906 it caused a twofold surprise. The report on the exercise says that enemy patrols were so astonished by the appearance of the armored car that they were completely paralysed. As a result the car crew were able to drive unhindered so close to the enemy's positions that they could find out all about his troops. The car's success in this its first mission was capped by the part it played in the capture of a Major-General commanding an enemy brigade.

A report on the manoeuvres of 1910 records an event which was to have a major impact on the future of the armored car as equipment for the German and Austrian armies: "The Austrian autumn manoeuvres took an unexpected turn. A young lieutenant, Count Schönfeldt, completely ruined the whole concept when he took advantage of the permission he had been granted to present the armored car he and Paul Daimler had built. The Emperor and his Generals were observing the course of the battle from a low hill. They were dismayed by messages informing them that the enemy's armored car had entered a well fortified village unhindered and even carried out a reconnaissance because evidently its appearance had been a total surprise. Such a thing was unheard of and broke all the rules of the war game. However, it gave the more thoughtful officers matter for meditation: they asked themselves whether the crazy machine might not in the last analysis be a useful instrument of war. There is no saying what might have happened in the next war if the decision had been taken to develop the new weapon and use armored regiments in place of cavalry, which is no less delicate than decorative. But the decision was left to the horses themselves. When the young lieutenant drove past the Generals' knoll in his puffing, clanking, smoke-belching vehicle, the highborn chargers on which the noble, gold-belted assembly were watching the manoeuvre began to tremble. The Emperor's gentle mount even attempted to bolt. That was the end of the new weapon..."

The Germans too overlooked the potentialities of the armored car, whose importance was not realized until well into the first world war, which broke out a few years later. This is what General Guderian, the famous German tank commander, has to say about the fatal sins of omission and erroneous judgments for which the German military establishment was responsible: "Trials were made with armored cars as early as the year 1909. Two French armored cars reached Eydtkunen by train on their way to Russia. The Russians did not take them over, so they were purchased by Germany. They took part in a manoeuvre of the 5th Brigade of Foot Guards with other motor vehicles. A report says: 'The armored cars can cover long distances very fast but have to keep to metalled roads. The speed—15 miles an hour—was too high and often had to be reduced to 4–8 miles an hour.' Although the Research Branch of the Transport Corps Inspectorate wanted to proceed with the construction of an armored car, the War Ministry decided on March 12, 1910, to desist from further experiments. It was considered that their field of application was very restricted: armored cars could only

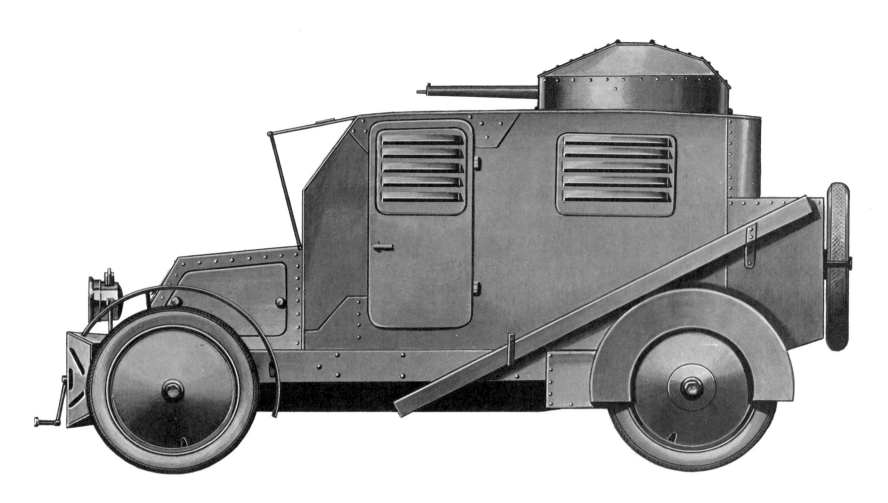

The armored car built by the French firm of Charron, Girardot and Voigt (CGV). Some cars of the series built in 1908 (CGV 1908) were to have been delivered to Russia. When they reached the German-Russian frontier they were not taken up so Germany bought them. But they were not greatly appreciated in German military circles.

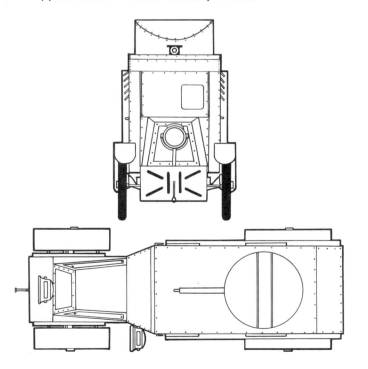

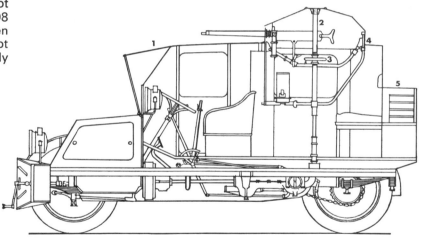

1 Steel plates hinged for better visibility. A second search-light was housed inside the vehicle behind a special shutter. The U-sections carried on the sides of the car were used as bridges for crossing trenches, waterways etc.
2 The turret was mounted on a column firmly anchored to the chassis.
3 A handwheel served to raise and lower the turret. When the turret was raised the machine gun could be aimed in all directions.
4 A rubber gasket prevented the turret from revolving when firing.
5 Ammunition magazine.

Armored car Erhardt-BAK (anti-balloon cannon) 1906. The Erhardt firm's armored car was the sensation of the 1906 Berlin Salon. It was a vehicle intended to combat balloons and airships and was equipped with a 5-pdr QF cannon.

prove militarily useful for frontier defense, in the mountains, and for blowing up bridges over waterways. That killed the armored car problem once and for all... ."

Nonetheless, the German High Command was well aware that armored combat cars were being developed in other countries. Moreover, thanks in part to the simultaneous improvement in communications media, such as press, wireless and cinema, it was now far easier to keep abreast of the latest technological achievements in every field. It may be that at the turn of the century the

The two classic structural features, internal-combustion engine and caterpillar track, were combined for the first time in the "land torpedoboat" designed by the Austrian sapper Burstyn in 1911. The design specified four jibs fore and aft for crossing deep trenches. The 60-h.p. power plant would have given a top speed on the road of 20 m.p.h. Travelling across country—the track enabled it to cope with any terrain —Burstyn's vehicle would not have done more than 5 m.p.h. At the time technical difficulties prevented the building of a demonstration prototype and ultimately the plan, which the military authorities had rejected, was consigned to oblivion.

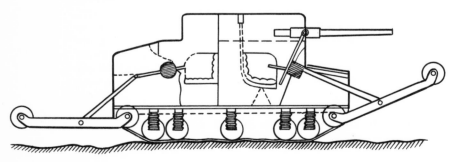

"rift" between the officer corps and civilian society in Germany had become too wide to be bridged. In any case, the military were as a rule more interested in maintaining ancient traditions and conventions than in a technologically orientated improvement and modernization of the armed forces. When we recall that during the first weeks of World War I officers fell because they considered it "dishonorable" to take cover from rifle and artillery fire, we can realize how strong must have been the resistance in the immediate prewar period to the introduction of the "ignoble" combat vehicle with protective armor.

Yet, when in 1913, for the first time in the history of war, the Italians employed armor-plated motorcars against Tripoli and their monstrous, high-wheeled Bianchis gave a good account of themselves in battle, there was no more stopping the development of the armored car on the European continent. The Germans finally formulated their own plan but it cannot be termed far-reaching. A four-wheel vehicle equipped with sheet steel armor and mounting a heavy machine gun was to have been built in 1913 at the request of the High Command in order to give mobility in open country to machine-gun detachments formed in about 1900. After the outbreak of World War I this plan led to the formation of the first German motor-cycle rifle units, which exceeded all expectations as regards speed and overland mobility. As a result of the first military successes the psychological resistance to the new combat vehicle was gradually overcome. For many officers, particularly those of the younger generation, exchanging the saddle for the commander's seat in a reconnaissance car ceased to amount to demotion. But the real breakthrough for the new weapon came later when the majority of tank corps officers were recruited from the once so aristocratic, privileged cavalry. If the changeover occurred without loss of face that was not only because the military duties of cavalry and tank corps were very similar but still more because there was no denying that tank troops enjoyed a very good "image". Today, when the "modern" history of armor covers a span of seventy years, the question remains as to whether it would not have been better for tank troops to be viewed, organized and employed as "technical units". The ensuing decades provide innumerable examples of outstanding actions by individual tank commanders, who often succeeded in achieving decisive successes by a single stroke of genius. But the outcome of the tank engagements during the last war proves that the tank was not the least important factor in the evolution of a type of warfare in which victory or defeat depends less and less on military or soldierly performance in the field and more and more on the economic and technological potential behind the lines in a country or a group of allied countries.

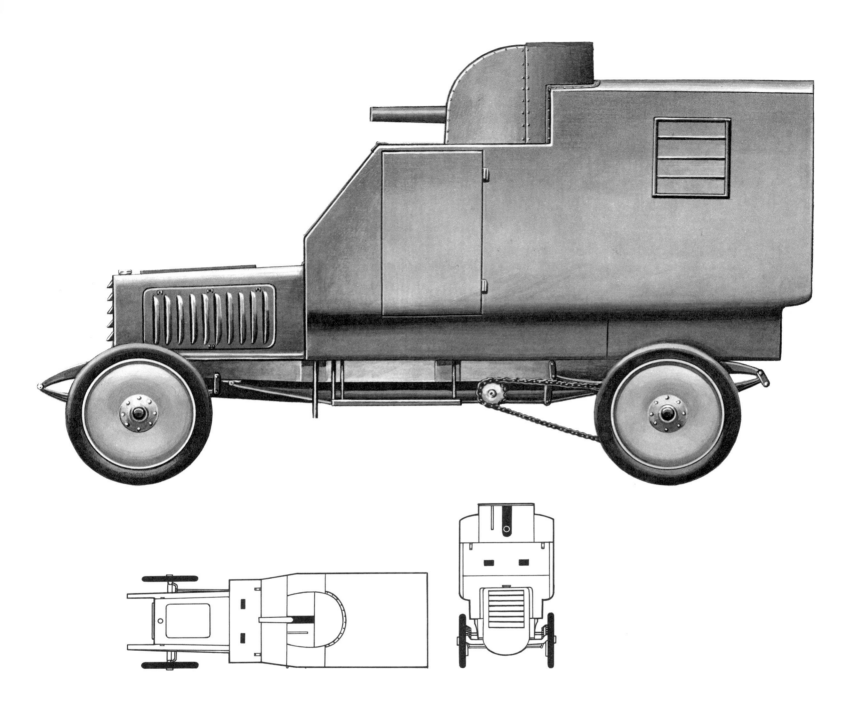

Armored Car, Erhardt-BAK   **(Germany)**
(Balloon destroyer)

Weight	3.5 short tons, 3.13 long tons
Engine	60 h.p. petrol engine
Speed	28 m.p.h. (45 km.p.h.)
Armament . . .	1 50-mm anti-balloon cannon L/30 in., traversing mount, Model 1906
Ammunition . .	100 rds
Range	2–5 miles (4–8 km)
Crew	5
Number in series .	Several
Year	1906

"Armor that does not protect is so much dead weight." That is what a Viennese newspaper had to say in 1907 about the Erhardt armored car built in Germany and equipped with a 50-mm anti-balloon gun (BAK 1906). Its armor plating was less than $1/8$ inch thick, but that was not the only defect that warranted criticism. Though the vehicle was designed for fighting balloons, its cannon could revolve through only a very small angle. The turret of the Austrians' own Austro-Daimler revolved through 360 degrees.

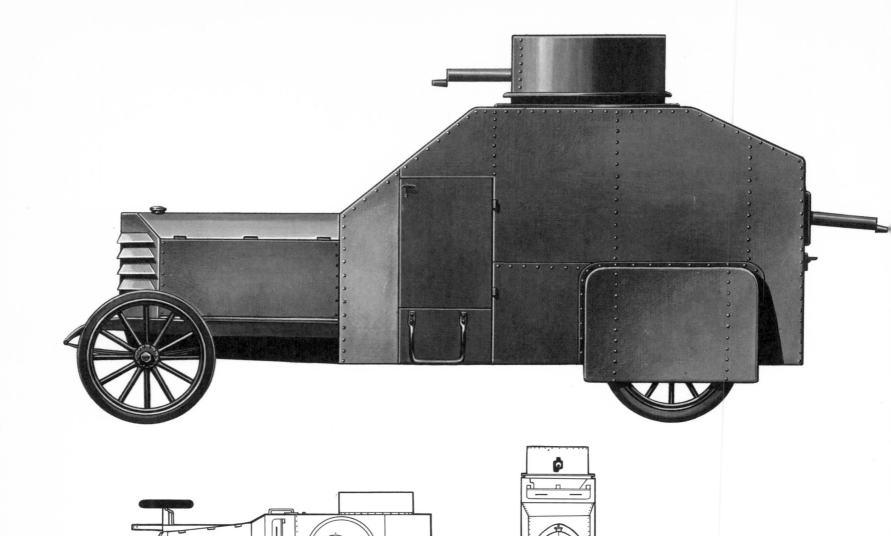

Bianchi Armored Car   (Italy)

Weight	3.4 short tons, 3.03 long tons (3.09 tons)
Length	14 ft. 9½ in. (4.5 m)
Width	5 ft. 11 in. (1.8 m)
Height	8 ft. 2½ in. (2.5 m)
Engine	30 h.p., watercooled
Speed	29 m.p.h. (46 km.p.h.)
Armament . . .	2 mg, 1 in the turret, 1 at the back
Crew	3–4
Year	1913

The first armored cars that ever saw action were built by
the makers of the Italian Bianchi motorcars. This vehicle,
which dates from 1914, was produced in large numbers.

World War I 3

Achtung Panzer! is the title of a book published in the 1930s by Major-General Heinz Guderian. It describes —from the German angle—the development of the modern tank, its tactical use, and its new operational potentialities in the field. The German "Tank General" begins with a detailed description of a cavalry engagement between Germans and Belgians in World War I. Three times the Germans—true to their theory of warfare and the tactics based thereon—charged the enemy, who were all dismounted and fought with rifles and machine guns. The German horsemen, attacking conventionally, suffered heavy losses and were repulsed again and again. "The first large-scale attempt," as Guderian says, "to charge modern weapons with cold steel had failed."

It was no mere chance that a tank general began a book on the tank with the description of a confrontation that was something new in the history of war—the confrontation between men armed in the traditional manner, fighting singly or in groups, and automatic weapons.

The foot soldiers in World War I were not spared the same experience and the same heavy losses as those cavalrymen in Belgium. Before a horseman could draw his sword, before a grenadier could fire a single aimed shot or his section fire a volley, they came within range of the machine guns, which were still watercooled in those days. The foolhardy leaving of cover was merely the first step towards the birch-wood cross that marks a soldier's grave. No wonder that within a few weeks the fighting was brought to a total standstill on almost every front. The lines became and remained so rigid that both sides hit upon the absurd idea of literally digging their way under the no-man's-land in order to avoid the risk of fighting above ground. As a matter of fact, the sappers chalked up several spectacular successes when, unseen by the enemy, they packed their underground galleries with explosives and blew great gaps in the enemy's system of fortified trenches. This makes it all the more surprising that the military men who excogitated such "tactics of desperation" did not speed up the development of the weapon that was to make a decisive impact not so much on the war itself as on the theory of warfare, which it changed completely. The tank, which made its first appearance half way through the war, succeeded before hostilities came to a close in steering military thinking into entirely new channels. From the technological viewpoint the concept of the modern tank was no novelty and industry was actually in a position to deliver combat vehicles capable of being employed in the field. What had previously been lacking was a military situation that would have favoured and finally called for a decisive step. A significant fact is that the 1914–18 war produced not only new, revolutionary weapons and methods but also an entirely new concept of war, in which enthusiasm for the participation of the whole nation in the military action had no place.

A *German Military History* published in 1966 summarizes these ideas in a passage on World War I. It says: "The first world war developed into total war, for the outcome of which the capacity of armament industry and food administration was the decisive factor; it ended with the collapse of the old Europe. After a few short weeks of an advance at breath-taking speed, a deadlock was reached where the belligerents exhausted themselves in the battles of material resources of 1916/18 in a hopeless attempt to achieve an operational breakthrough and so restore mobility in the open field. What failed was intellectually the mastery of technical details and tactically the conquest of a defensive belt 6 miles wide on either side. It was only with the tank in 1917 that a means was found to revolutionize the conduct of the war."

For some years—and those years subsequently had a decisive impact on warfare in general—the history of

(continued on page 38)

33

When the Germans launched their surprise attack in 1914, the Belgians sought to defend themselves with improvised armored cars. They fitted standard Rolls-Royce touring cars with steel plates at front and sides for protection against light artillery and equipped them with machine guns. The great success of these vehicles inspired the British Navy to fit out a number of cars along the same lines. Subsequently several motor-cars were fitted with armored turrets and the entire top of the machine was steel-plated. The original idea was for these vehicles to co-operate tactically with reconnaissance planes, but they proved too slow for that. However, a Royal Naval Armored Car Division was set up with a total of about 180 cars. Since they were adapted civilian types of various makes, spare-part stores were a problem. Logistical difficulties threw a long shadow before them.

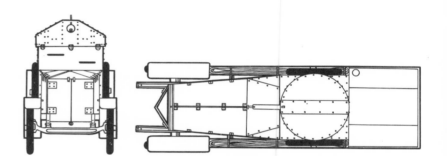

Armored Car, 1914 pattern   **(Great Britain)**
Rolls-Royce

Weight	3.9 short tons, 3.5 long tons (3.6 tons)
Length	16 ft. 9 in. (5.11 m)
Width	6 ft. 3 in. (1.9 m)
Height	7 ft. 7 in. (2.31 m)
Engine	Rolls-Royce, 6-cylinder, watercooled, 40–50 h.p.
Speed	60 m.p.h. (100 km.p.h.)
Range	150 miles (241.3 km)
Armament . . .	1×0.303 in. Maxim mg, later Vickers mg
Ammunition . .	3,000 mg rds
Armor	9 mm
Crew	3–4
Number in series .	About 82
Year	1914–15

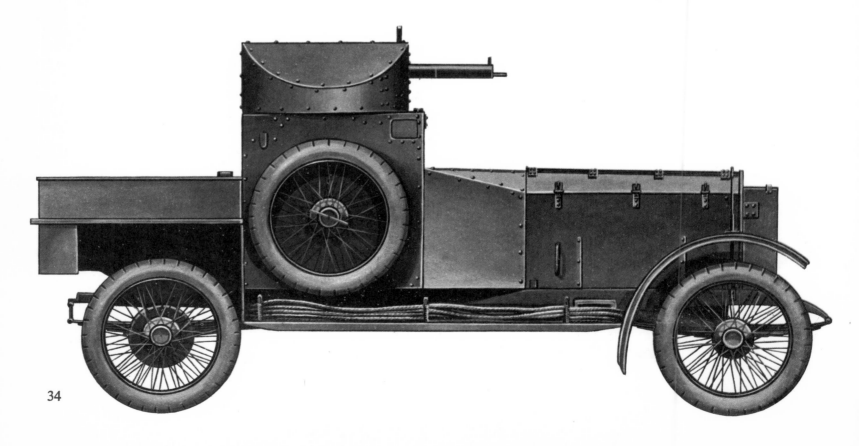

The Garford armored car built in America had a standard truck chassis and wheels with solid rubber tires. It weighed over 10½ tons, which made it very cumbersome, and was powered by a 35-h.p. engine. It saw service in Russia, Estonia and Poland. Being considered too heavy for American roads, and probably for Russian roads too, it was put on railway tracks and used as an armored rail trolley.

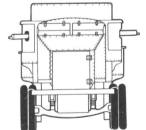

Armored Car, Garford (U.S.A.)

Weight	12.1 short tons, 10.8 long tons (11 tons)
Length	18 ft. 8 ½ in. (5.7 m)
Width	7 ft. 6 ½ in. (2.3 m)
Height	9 ft. 2 in. (2.8 m)
Speed	11–19 m.p.h. (18–30 km.p.h.)
Armament . . .	1 cannon, 3 mg
Armor	7–9 mm
Crew	8
Year	1915–17

Lanchester armored cars went through many adventures in World War I. Thirty or forty were sent to France in 1915 and at the end of the same year a certain number of them attempted to reach Russia via the Arctic route under Commander Oliver Locker-Lampson but failed to do so. After the inevitable repairs they were dispatched to Persia, Turkey, the Caucasus and Rumania. The Lanchesters were lighter than the Rolls-Royces and covered more miles than any other combat vehicle used in World War I.

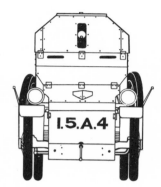

Armored Car, Lanchester   **(Great Britain)**

Weight	5.3 short tons, 4.8 long tons (4.9 tons)
Length	16 ft. (4.88 m)
Width.	6 ft. 4 in. (1.93 m)
Height	7 ft. 6 in. (2.29 m)
Engine	Lanchester, 6-cylinder, 60 h.p.
Speed.	50 m.p.h. (80 km.p.h.)
Range.	180 miles (290 km)
Armament . . .	1 × 0.303 in. Vickers mg
Ammunition . .	3,000 mg rds
Armor	8 mm
Crew	4
Number in series.	About 36
Year	1915

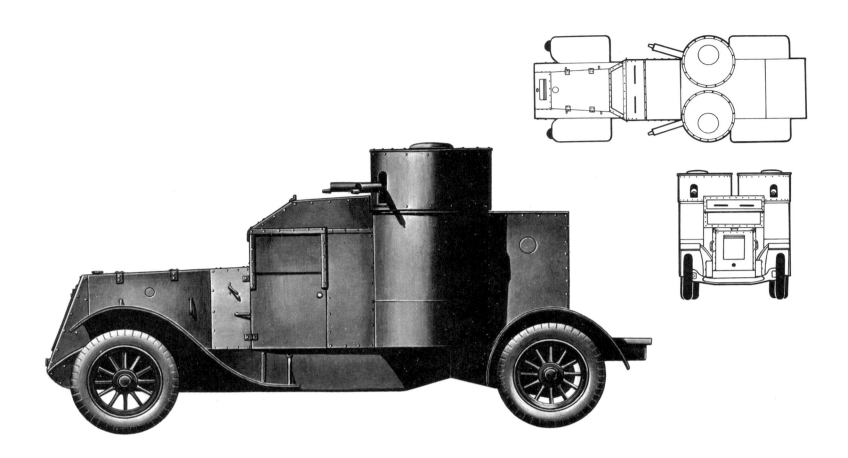

The Austin armored car was based on a truck chassis. Like many of the other types built in the West at that time, it was supplied to the Russian army from 1915 on. In 1917 it was equipped with a second steering wheel at the rear, but it still had only one (slow) reverse gear and the front wheels alone could be steered. So it really did not warrant the claim that it could run in both directions.

Armored Car, Austin (Great Britain)

Weight	4.6–5.8 short tons, 4.1–5.2 long tons (4.2–5.3 tons)
Length	15 ft. 7 in.–16 ft. 0 ¾ in. (4.75–4.9 m)
Width	6 ft. 6 in.–6 ft. 8 in. (1.95–2.03 m)
Height	7 ft. 10 ½ in. (2.4 m)
Engine	Austin, 4-cylinder, watercooled, 50 h.p.
Speed	31 m.p.h. (50 km.p.h.)
Tank capacity . .	19.02 U.S. gal., 15.9 Imp. gal. (72 l)
Range	125 miles (201 km)
Armament . . .	2 × 0.303 in. Maxim mg or 2 Hotchkiss mg
Ammunition . .	5,000–6,000 rds
Armor	6–8 mm
Crew	4–5
Number in series .	Produced in large numbers
Year	1915–17

N.B. Produced in two forms, accounting for dimensional differences.

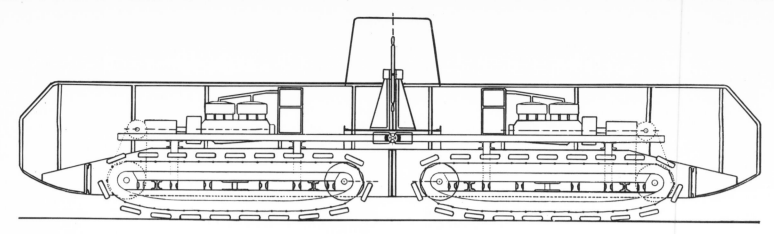

Project of a British landship on caterpillar tracks. This vehicle would have been over 30 feet long and have weighed about 24 tons. Its design was based on experience with submarines and armored cars. Captain (later Admiral) Murray Sueter, head of the Royal Naval Air Service, submitted his project to the British Landship Committee for approval on March 4, 1915. Outstanding features of the design were the tall bow and stern and two pairs of tracks. At that time the tank industry was not capable of manufacturing tracks that were at once long and reliable.

tank-like combat vehicles equipped with internal-combustion engines and steel armor plating was a chapter of British military history. Like so many other periods and phases in the military history of every country, the evolution of military policy in Britain was peppered with affairs, scandals and intrigues. At the beginning of the century the Austrian Emperor's horse had shied at the puffing, clanking Daimler, and "horse sense" had kept Austria from building armored cars. After the same fashion private feuds, inter-service jealousy and, last but not least, political give and take were decisive factors in the development of the British tank. Today, thanks to the recollections of a great many politicians, technicians and military officers who took part in the construction of the first tanks, we are in a position to reconstruct the course of events with a certain precision. There are, of course, flaws and inconsistencies in this history of the "tank years", for many a bitter opponent of that "useless and unserviceable fancy weapon" did all they could a few years later to be counted among the shrewd, far-seeing "fathers of the tank".

It was in October 1914 that three British officers first discussed in real earnest the possibility of developing a

new war machine that would combine all the latest technological achievements. Colonel (later General) Sir Ernest Dunlop Swinton, posted to France as military attaché, Lieutenant-Colonel Sir Maurice (later Lord) Hankey and Captain T.G. Tulloch debated the question whether the American Holt tractor then used for artillery traction could be transformed into a combat vehicle and employed for attacking enemy machine-gun nests. Hankey submitted the idea to the War Minister, Lord Kitchener, who rejected it out of hand.

Shortly after, in December of the same year, Hankey made another attempt. This time he suggested building the machine as an infantry-support weapon. Like the Holt Caterpillar Tractor, the steel-plated vehicle would be able to climb over or break through trenches and pulverize barbed wire entanglements thanks to its endless tread. It would also offer protection to advancing infantrymen.

Paradoxically enough, though not conceived as an armed combat car, this vehicle met with greater success than Swinton's more advanced project. A copy of Hankey's paper happened to reach Winston Churchill, who was First Lord of the Admiralty at the time. He passed

L. A. de Mole, an Australian engineer from North Adelaide, had already submitted in 1912 and 1915 an "endless belt" design to the War Office. It even incorporated front axle steering. The War Office showed no interest whatever.

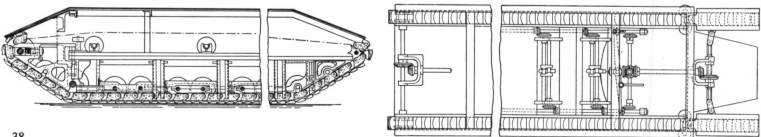

it on to the Prime Minister, Herbert Asquith, recommending its adoption. Churchill had already ordered armored cars for the defense of a seaplane base at Dunkirk and wanted to equip those roadbound wheeled vehicles with portable bridges.

Churchill in fact carried Hankey's idea one step farther and suggested the construction of steam-powered vehicles based on the Holt Caterpillar system, equipped with armor plating and a heavy machine gun, which would drive through the enemy's lines under cover of night. The Prime Minister passed the suggestion on—or, rather, back—to Lord Kitchener, who this time found it more to his liking and made arrangements for trials with tractors specially built for the purpose. The outcome was the appearance of the first "machine-gun destroyer", an excessively heavy track-laying machine that was presented to a number of military observers in February 1915 and proved a failure. It is true that far too much was demanded of it; but the whole idea seemed preposterous to some important personages in the War Ministry. They had never liked it, so they purely and simply let it drop.

But the Admiralty had not lost interest. A certain Commodore Hetherington, transport officer for the wheeled armored units, studied the feasibility of building a "landship" that would carry 36-cm cannon and have three gigantic turrets with six 12-cm guns each. To bear the huge weight of the superstructure, the landship would have measured about 115 feet in length and over 65 feet in breadth. The plan provided for a track-laying model in addition to the original wheeled design. It soon became evident, however, that such monstrous vehicles could not possibly perform the tasks for which they were intended.

Nonetheless, the Admiralty and the recently established Ministry of Munitions co-operated in the search for other, more serviceable combat vehicles. Support also came from another quarter—the firm of William Foster & Company, of Lincoln. The arrival on the scene of a civilian enterprise meant that the new weapon presented not only a military but also an economic interest. By now the Army had clearly formulated their requirements. In their view the new combat vehicles should be sufficiently armored to provide sure protection against infantry fire. They should be able to traverse vertical obstacles up to about 4 feet high and cross trenches 11 feet wide. Three different armored vehicles were built but none of these prototypes was ever used in the field. Nevertheless, they provided essential experience for the first production machines. Today some of the features of those British-built prototypes are still incorporated in tanks of various origin. Fosters had already built large wheeled vehicles for transporting heavy guns and could also count on a certain experience in armored car manufacture. Since

time was short, the power plant and transmission system were taken over from existing wheeled models.

About that time Swinton, who deserves to be called the first theorist of tank technology, wrote a memorandum mentioning the "moral" effect of the tank, on which much emphasis was laid later. More important still, he warned against employing tanks in insufficient numbers.

The prospects of success of a tank offensive, he said, resided mainly in the surprise factor; thus a repeat performance could not offer the same chances of success

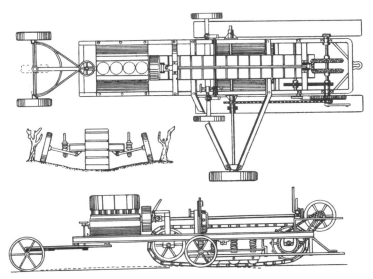

The American Holt Tractor Company built a tractor with track and wheel drive. After acquiring patents owned by the British firm of Ruston Hornsby and Sons, Holt built partly armored tractors for the U.S. artillery.

An "idea on tracks". This armored car superstructure with revolving turret was mounted on an American Killen Strait track-laying chassis. The vehicle was demonstrated before Lloyd George, at that time British Minister of Munitions. Its successful presentation marked the real start of systematic tank development in England.

as the initial, unexpected attack. The machines should not be used in driblets as they were delivered from the factory but their existence should be kept secret until a large-scale operation co-ordinated with a infantry attack could be envisaged.

Two of Swinton's remarks should be given special attention. He voiced the opinion that tanks should not be employed "in driblets". This means that he wanted to increase the impact of the new weapon by massing together a large number of tanks in order to achieve a decisive penetration and breakthrough of the enemy's lines. This view seems to have been consigned to oblivion for a great many years. It is true that General Charles de Gaulle, who, when still a captain, took an interest in the development and utilization of the tank, formulated the same considerations as to the thorough-going employment of massed tanks. But that doctrine was not accepted until

long after the outbreak of World War II. However, General Guderian agreed with Swinton's caution against employing tanks "in driblets" when he issued the directive still remembered by German tank corps cadets today: "Don't dribble, pour!"

Swinton's second warning concerned secrecy, which in his eyes was a necessary condition for the success of the weapon. If his first requirement—the massed use of a large number of tanks—was not taken seriously, his call for secrecy did not fall on deaf ears. In order to prevent enemy spies in Britain and abroad from finding out about the technical and tactical preparations then under way, the prototype tanks were given a misleading code name which, describing as it did something that actually existed, was eminently suited to distract attention from the real objective. At that time gigantic steel cisterns were under construction for holding water supplies for British colonial

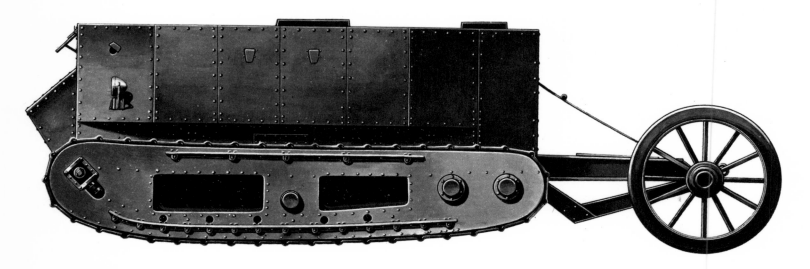

"Little Willie" was an experimental tank that made its first trial run in September 1915. Equipped with different types of tracks, it did not prove satisfactory. The chassis was too short and too high and the vehicle had difficulty in traversing trenches more than four feet wide. But King George V had seen it and other types of tank were designed and built with his approval.

"Little Willie"   **(Great Britain)**

Height	10 ft. 2 in (3.2 m)
Engine	Daimler, 105 h.p.
Speed	2 m.p.h. (3 km.p.h.)
Armament . . .	1 2-pdr cannon (never fitted)
Armor	10 mm
Year	1915

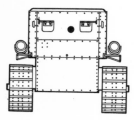

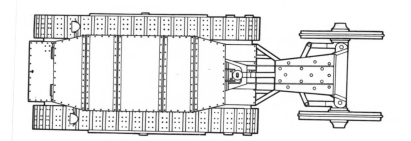

"Little Willie" built by Messrs William Foster and Company of Lincoln was an improved version of the first Tritton machine.

forces operating in tropical regions. Only a few people were parties to the closely guarded secret that the word "tank" referred not to those cisterns but to mobile fighting machines that would spout fire instead of water. That is how the tank got its name. What is not yet quite clear is when and how news of the novel weapon first reached the German High Command. There is good reason to believe that it did not see the light until the first tanks, for all their technical shortcomings, reaped their first military or, rather, psychological successes.

The first prototype, "No. 1 Lincoln Machine", reached the drawing board in July 1915, was assembled in August and put through its first trials in September of the same year. It was a huge rectangular steel structure mounted on two lateral tracks driven by a 6-cylinder 105 h.p. Daimler engine. The 18-ton vehicle could do 2 miles an hour on the level, but that "speed" had to be greatly reduced whenever it had to climb an obstacle 18 inches high. The turret, which could rotate through 360 degrees, brought the overall height to about 11 feet. The plan was to equip it with a cannon and four machine guns. But for the trials it was fitted with a dummy turret of approximately the same weight. The experience gained with this machine led to its re-construction in a modified form, though it still closely resembled its predecessor. But "Little Willie",

as it was now known, which was ready later in September 1915, displayed substantial improvements in the design of track and driving wheels. For instance, the span of the track was increased to about 13 feet, giving the vehicle better road-holding and considerably improving its cross-country capability. The driving wheels were fitted with projecting steel lugs that provided better guidance for the track members and prevented their slipping off sideways.

However, a third prototype named "Mother", of which only a single specimen was built, was necessary before a model suitable for mass production was found. Its major innovation was an entirely new silhouette. "Mother" was the model for the first production tank, known as Mark I. Trials with "Little Willie" had proved that the vehicle's cross-country capability was much reduced if the height was too great and the track too narrow. Consequently, "Mother" embodied an attempt to increase the span of the track and diminish the overall height. The result was the well-known lozenge-shaped hull with raised driving wheels in front and the track encircling the entire profile. Trials with the prototypes had made it clear that as far as possible the track must be the first part to contact the obstacle if the climbing operation was to succeed. "Mother" provided a perfect solution of this problem, which is why all British tanks built up to the end of World War I

(continued on page 44)

41

A marine by the name of Hill attached to the Royal Naval Air Service drove the "Mother" tank for the first time at Hatfield Park north of London in January, 1916. After a number of additions and alterations, this model was sent into action on the deadlocked Western front. Many observers view the appearance of the tank as the turning point of the war: the British High Command had recognized the signs of the times and the appearance of the first tank on the field of battle meant that technology and economic power had become the preponderant factors. The call "Tanks in Sight!" struck terror into the heart of the footsoldier.

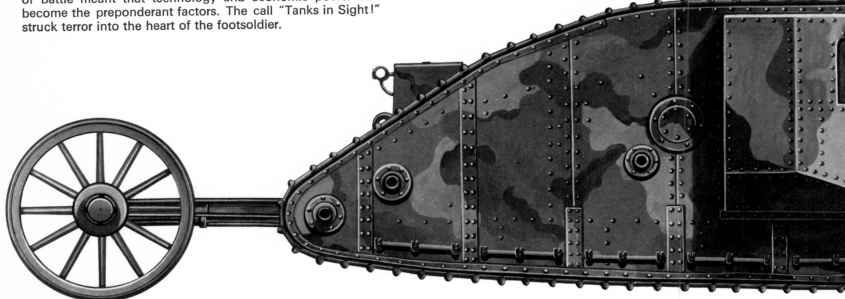

Tank, Mark I   **(Great Britain)**

Weight	31.3 short tons, 28 long tons (male) (28.5 tons)
	30.1 short tons, 27 long tons (female) (27.4 tons)
Length	32 ft. 6 in. (with "steering" wheels) (9.90 m)
Width	13 ft. 9 ½ in. (4.2 m) (male)
	14 ft. 4 ½ in. (4.38 m) (female)
Height	8 ft. 2 in. (2.49 m)
Engine	Daimler, 6-cylinder, watercooled 105 h.p., 1,000 r.p.m.
Speed	4 m.p.h. (6 km.p.h.)
Tank capacity . .	About 52.85 U.S. gal., 44 Imp. gal. (200 l)
Range	24 miles (38 km)
Armament . . .	2 40-caliber 6 pdr cannon, 4 mg Hotchkiss (male); 4 Vickers 0.303 in. mg, 1 mg Hotchkiss (female)
Ammunition . .	324–32 6 pdr, 6,000–31,232 mg rds
Armor	12 mm
Crew	8
Number in series .	100
Year	1916

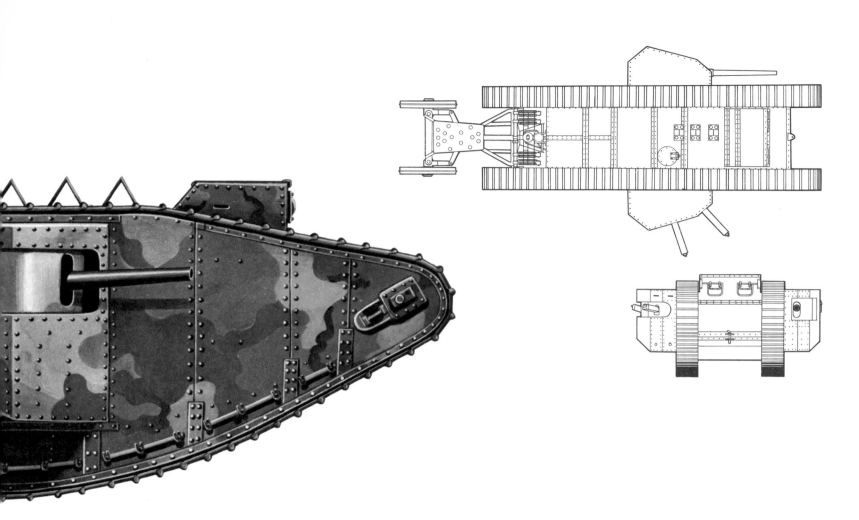

The shape of the British "Mother" armored vehicle justified the code name "water tank" it was given, as shown in this picture of the Mark 1.

During the last two years of World War I 400 Schneider CA 1 (M 16) tanks were supplied to the French army. The first saw action at the Chemin des Dames in April 1917 during the Somme offensive.

kept to the principle of the over-all track. "Mother" was put through the first run under its own power on January 13, 1916, over a course laid down exactly according to the measurements of the German fortified positions in France. A week later "Mother" fired the first shot with its cannon, which were mounted in sponsons on each side; they had already been tested by the Navy. Next, the armor was tested with captured German machine guns firing German ammunition against the steel plates on the front of the machine. The fact that a great many 5-cm guns had been taken in overrun German positions led people to fear that the enemy already possessed small-calibre antitank weapons. This assumption proved wrong, at least when tanks were first employed in the field. In February 1916 "Mother" was put through its paces in the presence of a select group of British politicians. Most of them were convinced of the value of the new weapon, but the War Minister, Lord Kitchener, resolutely maintained his opinion that the machine could not win a war. Meanwhile a group of experienced "motorists" had been

assembled: they later formed the backbone of the British Tank Corps. At the end of 1915 the "Heavy Section of the Machine Gun Corps" had been formed under Colonel Swinton's command.

The original program provided for the building of a hundred Mark I tanks, production machines developed from "Mother". For tactical reasons the program was divided into two parts and the order finally issued was for 75 "male" and 75 "female" Mark Is, which differed only in their armament. The tactical plan was that the male Mark I equipped with two cannon mounted in lateral sponsons would drive the enemy troops out of their trenches with long-range fire, after which the female version, which was equipped solely with machine guns, would take care of the soldiers on the run.

Before a single production machine was ready for action, Sir Douglas Haig, Supreme British Commander in France, demanded tanks for the offensive on the Somme planned for summer 1916. As a matter of fact, the first few tanks reached the front just as the attack was about to be

(continued on page 49)

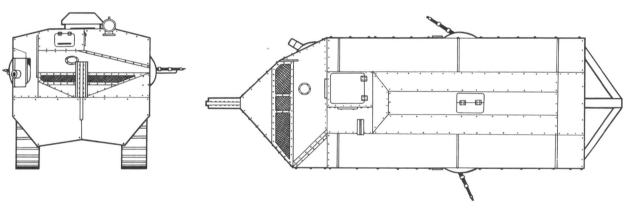

Tank, Schneider M.16 CA1   **(France)**

Weight	14.9 short tons, 12.9 long tons (13.5 tons)
Length	19 ft. 7 in. (5.97 m)
Width	10 ft. 9 in. (3.28 m)
Height	7 ft. 8 in. (2.34 m)
Engine	Schneider, 4-cylinder, watercooled, 55 h.p. (8 km.p.h.)
Speed	4 ½ m.p.h. (6 km.p.h.)
Tank capacity . .	53 U.S. gal., 44.1 Imp. gal. (201 l)
Range	25 miles (40 km)
Armament . . .	1 75-mm Howitzer, 2 Hotchkiss mg
Ammunition . .	90 75-mm rds, 4,400 Hotchkiss rds
Armor	11.5 mm (+8 mm on later vehicles)
Crew	6–7
Number in series .	400
Year	1916–17

In 1916 the French firm of Schneider brought out their CA1 tank. Though it had been developed independently of the British model, it bore a strong outer resemblance to "Little Willie". The French army had ordered 400 but only 132 were ready when they went into action for the first time at the Chemin des Dames in April 1917. Besides certain structural defects, their armor plating was too weak and the fire hazard was far too great. In this respect they were very vulnerable even to light artillery fire. The second batch of Schneider tanks was a great improvement on the first.

The St. Chamond tank, another French model, was almost twice as heavy as the Schneider. It held a crew of nine, five of whom served the cannon and machine guns. Four hundred tanks of this model were built. Some were sent to the Western front in May 1917; others were shipped to Russia.

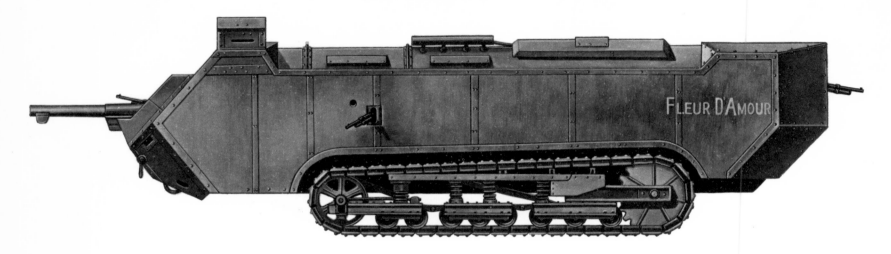

On the whole the French St. Chamond tank gave better results than the Schneider, but its hull projected far beyond the tracks making it very unwieldy for cross-country work.

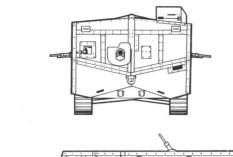

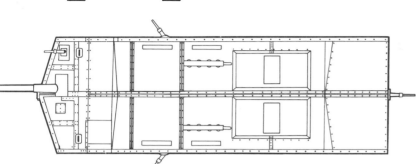

Tank, St. Chamond M.16   (France)

Weight	25.3 short tons, 22.6 long tons (23 tons)
Length	25 ft. 11 in. (7.91 m)
Width	8 ft. 9 in. (2.67 m)
Height	7 ft. 8 in. (2.34 m)
Engine	Panhard, 4-cylinder, watercooled, 90 h.p.
Speed	5 m.p.h. (8 km.p.h.)
Tank capacity .	66 U.S. gal., 55 Imp. gal. (250 l)
Range	37 miles (60 km)
Armament . . .	1 75-mm Model 1897 cannon, 4 mg
Ammunition . .	106 75-mm rds, 7,500 Hotchkiss rds
Armor	17 mm
Crew	9
Number in series .	400
Year	1916–17

Only one model of the German Büssing armored car was actually built. It was employed in 1915 and gave an adequate performance. It weighed 10 tons, was manned by a crew of nine and thanks to its 90-h.p. engine had a top speed of 25 m.p.h. Its operational radius was 156 miles.

Armored Car, Büssing A5P   (Germany)

Weight	11.28 short tons, 10.09 long tons (10.25 tons)
Length	31 ft. 2 in. (9.5 m)
Width	6 ft. 11 in. (2.1 m)
Engine	Büssing, 6-cylinder, watercooled, 90 h.p.
Speed	25 m.p.h. (40 km.p.h.)
Range	156 miles (250 km)
Armament . . .	3–5 mg
Armor	5–7 mm
Crew	9
Number in series .	One only
Year	1915

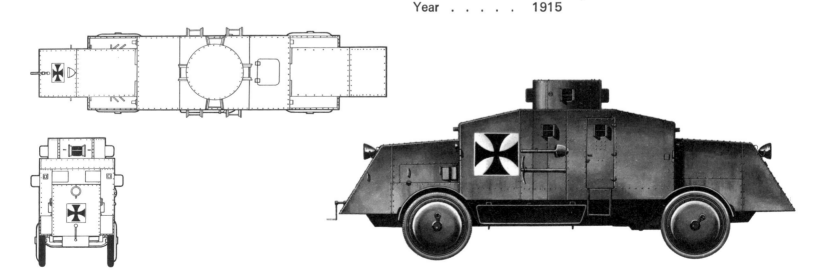

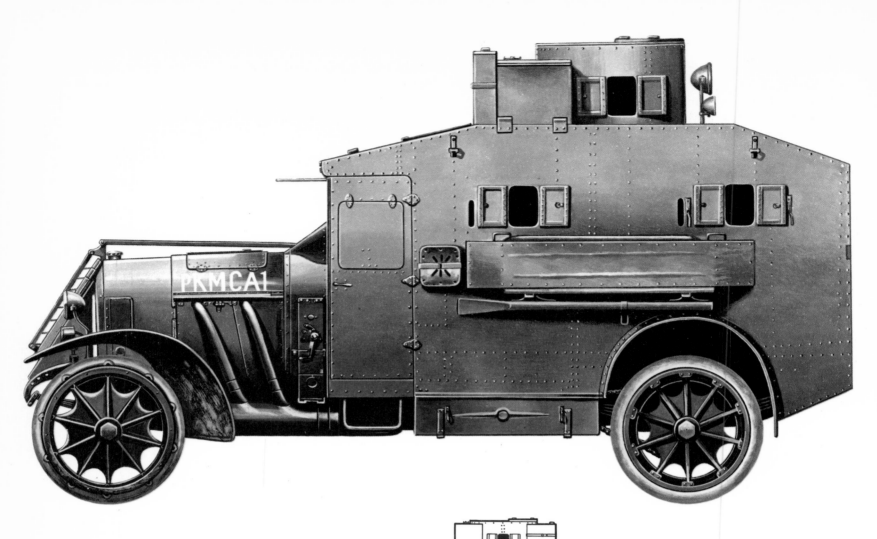

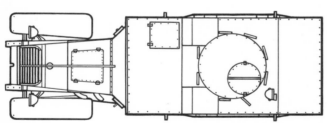

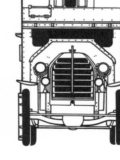

Armored Car, Daimler   **(Germany)**

Weight	9.65 short tons, 8.61 long tons (8.75 tons)
Length	18 ft. 5 in. (5.61 m)
Width	6 ft. 9 in. (2.05 m)
Engine	Daimler M 1464, 4-cylinder, watercooled, 60–80 h.p., 850–1,200 r.p.m.
Speed	24 m.p.h. (forwards) (38 km.p.h.) 20 m.p.h. (backwards) (33 km.p.h.)
Armor	7 mm
Armament . . .	3 mg
Range	155 miles (248 km)
Crew	8–9
Number in series .	One only (and two similar)
Year	1915

The Daimler armored car of 1915 fitted with Krupp steel plating was also built in one model only. The German High Command was not greatly interested. It was manned by a crew of eight and measured about 17 feet in length but its twin steering gear made it extremely flexible. It could do almost 24 m.p.h. forwards and over 20 in reverse. Like the Büssing, the Daimler was used to good effect by the German troops in Rumania in 1916.

48

launched. Swinton's fears of their being used "in driblets" were realized. The new tanks were called upon to demonstrate their serviceability before the order for a second large batch could be issued. The first British tank company landed in France in August. The men had given each machine a name that was painted on its sides. News of the arrival of the new, terrifying combat vehicle spread like wildfire: that was the end of the absolute secrecy Swinton had insisted on. The second company followed two days before the first company went into action. But before the third company arrived, the battle on the Somme had started and motor-powered, track-laying vehicles were employed for the first time in the history of war. Captain John Fuller, a British officer who later reached the rank of Major-General, has given a graphic description of a tank engagement. He recounts how out of the thirty machines put into action only one achieved its goal. Nineteen were

obstructed, five were hit and five others broke down. The ground was so thick with mud that some tanks narrowly escaped disappearing into the mire.

In his book General Guderian also criticizes the British for throwing away the chance of a surprise attack with massed tanks. But his account of the first engagement is far more favourable than Fuller's. He writes: "Despite their small number, they were split up and employed, part in General Rawlinson's 4th Army, part in General Gough's, which was kept in reserve. Though they were frittered away and some were eliminated, as was to be expected, the use of these few machines resulted in the greatest British success to date. This was due basically to the surprise appearance of the new weapon and boosted the morale of the British infantry at once."

War diaries mention a message radioed from a British reconnaissance plane: "A tank is advancing up Flers High

(continued on page 55)

The Canadian general, Odlum, in conversation on the road from Arras to Cambrai on September 2, 1918. His command tank is a French Renault FT 17.

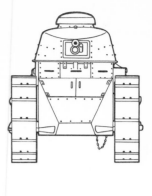

In July 1916, after much hesitation, the French motor-car manufacturer Louis Renault yielded to General Estienne's pressing demands and it was not long before the first Renault light tank was put to the test of battle. Its success in standing up to competition from other French and British tanks is demonstrated by the fact that vehicles of the same type with only a few minor improvements saw action in North Africa in 1942. It could be equipped at will with cannon or machine gun and its decisive advantage was its light weight —about 7 tons. This meant that it could be loaded on a truck and dispatched to the front ready for action. When the Renault FT 17 was subsequently equipped with a 37-mm gun, a periscope was also fitted. This gave the crew—the commander, who doubled as gunner, and the driver—an enormous advantage over the blind crew of heavier tanks. First employed in very small numbers, the Renault was amazingly successful towards the end of the war. In July 1918 a massive assault in which 480 Renaults were thrown into the fray cut a hole about four miles deep in the German defenses. This breakthrough, which had not been prepared by an artillery barrage, was not transformed into a decisive victory because the only reserves that could be thrown into the breach were the French cavalry, an arm that had long been given up as useless by both sides.

Light Tank, Renault FT 17   **(France)**

Weight	8.1 short tons, 7.2 long tons (7.4 tons)
Length	16 ft. 5 in. (5 m)
Width	5 ft. 7 ½ in. (1.71 m)
Height	7 ft. (2.13 m)
Engine	Renault 95×160, 4-cylinder, watercooled, 35 h.p.
Speed	2–5 m.p.h. (3–8 km.p.h.)
Tank capacity . .	27.6 U.S. gal., 23 Imp. gal. (104.6 l)
Range	22 miles (35 km)
Armament . . .	1 37-mm gun
Ammunition . .	30 37-mm rds
Armor	6-22 mm
Crew	2
Number in series .	1,560 of all types
Year	1918

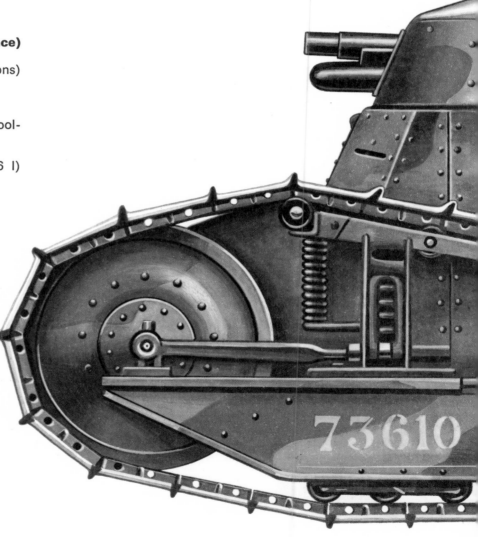

73610

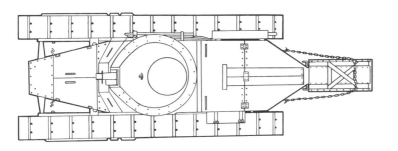

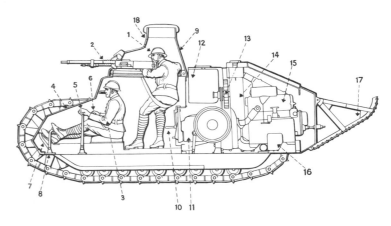

1, commander, machine gunner or gunner; 2, machine gun or cannon; 3, driver; 4, hatch; 5, steering lever; 6, gear lever; 7, brake; 8, accelerator; 9, hatch; 10, starting handle; 11, gearbox; 12, fuel tank; 13, fan; 14, radiator; 15, engine; 16, oil tank; 17, trench-crossing tail; 18, turret.

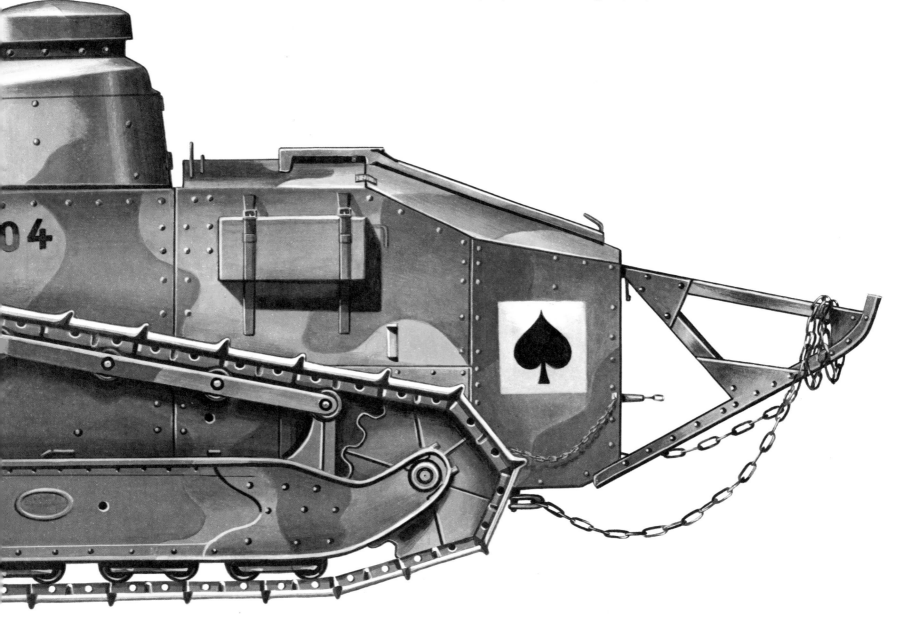

Tank, Mark IV   **(Great Britain)**

Weight	31.9 short tons, 28.5 long tons (male) (29 tons)
	30.8 short tons, 27.5 long tons (female) (28 tons)
Length	26 ft. 5 in. (8.05 m)
Width	12 ft. 9 ½ in. (male) (3.89 m)
	10 ft. 6 in. (female) (3.2 m)
Height	8 ft. 2 in. (2.49 m)
Engine	Daimler, 6-cylinder, watercooled, 105 h.p., later 125 h.p.
Speed	2–4 m.p.h. (3–6 km.p.h.)
Tank capacity . .	84 U.S. gal., 70 Imp. gal. (318 l)
Range	45 miles (72 km)
Armament . . .	2 6-pdr QF, 23 caliber, plus 3 Hotchkiss mg (male) or 6 Hotchkiss mg (female)
Ammunition . .	204 6-pdr rds, 5,640 rds mg (male) 12,972 rds (female)
Armor	6–16 mm
Crew	7
Number in series .	1,220
Year	1917–18

The first tank ever engaged in what might be termed a "classic" combat with another tank was a British Mark IV. On April 24, 1918, accompanied by two "female" tanks—i.e. tanks equipped with machine guns—it encountered one of the A7V tanks built by the Germans during the last months of the war. The British tank was victorious in this first tank duel but the German vehicle inflicted heavy damage on its two consorts. This experience persuaded the British makers to improve their equipment and many of the "female" tanks were fitted with adequate antitank guns.

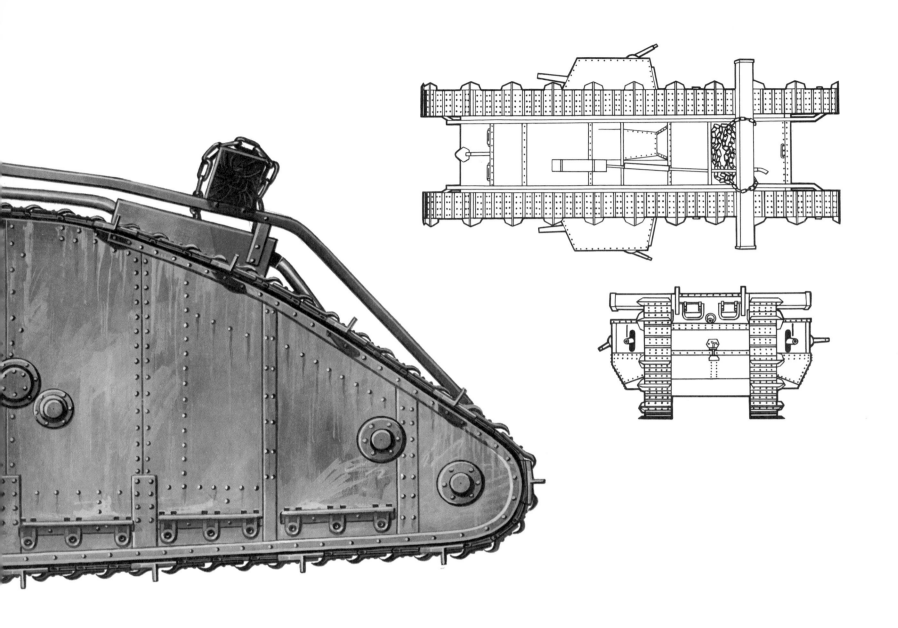

1, engine; 2, driver's seat; 3, fuel tank; 4, radiator; 5, tool-boxes; 6, front turret; 7, manhole turret; 8, water tank; 9, revolver case; 10, gearbox; 11, starting crank.

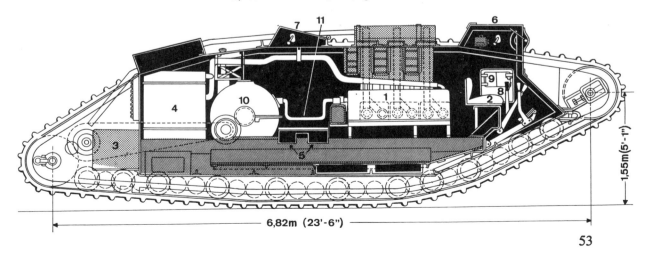

1.55m (5'-1")

6,82m (23'-6")

A British Mark V with the 4th battalion, 5th Royal Berkshire Regiment during the battle of Amiens in 1918.

More than 1000 Mark IVs were produced in Britain during the first war.

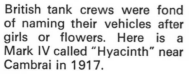

British tank crews were fond of naming their vehicles after girls or flowers. Here is a Mark IV called "Hyacinth" near Cambrai in 1917.

Street with the British Army cheering behind it." This made a great impression in England, so it is no wonder that the Government ordered a new series of tanks in view of individual successes which had an important psychological impact, if no other. This time the order was for a thousand. Although it was subsequently realized in official British quarters that Swinton was right to regret that "a surprise had been thrown away" when the first few tanks were employed, that deserving officer was put on the shelf. He was replaced by Colonel Hugh Elles, who commanded an infantry brigade.

The appearance of the first British tanks also startled the French, who had tried in vain to prevent the new weapon being employed until their own hastily built armored vehicles were ready to take the field. After many false starts Colonel Eugène Estienne finally succeeded in persuading the French High Command to order 400 tanks. Estienne was anxious for the order to be given to the Schneider company, which had already delivered their useful Schneider light armored car, and therefore could count on a certain experience in this field. But it was their competitors, St. Chamond, who were entrusted with the

task of building larger tanks designed to carry a field gun and four machine guns. When the first French tanks went into battle it was found that the Schneiders, being lighter, were far handier than the St. Chamonds, whose narrow tracks restricted their overland capability. It was only when Renault was persuaded to take an interest in tank construction that the French army got the light Renault tank, 1,150 of which were ordered at once. The success of the Renault FT 17 led the French High Command to order a total of 3,500 tanks, some of them from Schneider, Berliet and Delaunay-Belleville.

When the Americans came into the war they were so convinced of the importance of the new weapon that they ordered 1,200 from the French. The construction of 200 French radio tanks was an interesting development that made an important impact on the evolution of tank tactics. It was the first step towards the reconnaissance or command tank. By then the tank had acquired a preponderant influence on the military thinking of both the British and the French. The Germans seem, on the contrary, to have paid very slight attention to the new weapon. This is what an order of the Crown-Prince

(continued on page 61)

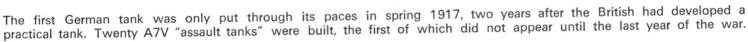

The first German tank was only put through its paces in spring 1917, two years after the British had developed a practical tank. Twenty A7V "assault tanks" were built, the first of which did not appear until the last year of the war.

The reason why the Germans lagged behind their opponents on the other side of the Channel can be discovered in the complicated code name of the first German tank. A7V stood for "Allgemeine Kriegsdepartement 7 Abteilung Verkehrswesen" (War Department General Division 7 Transport), the body responsible for tank development in the German Empire. The A7V had a crew of 18 and was equipped with a 57-mm cannon and six machine guns. It weighed 30 tons and its two 100-h.p. engines gave it a top speed of about 5 ½ m.p.h. On the whole it gave a good account of itself but only 20 were built and that was not enough to achieve a decisive victory towards the end of the war. Nonetheless, the A7V made a great impact on the subsequent development of the tank in Germany.

The tank corps needed practical uniforms. The crew of a German A7V tank wore leather helmets with splinterproof plaited steel masks.

Heavy Tank, A7V (Germany)

Weight	33 short tons, 29.5 long tons (30 tons)
Length	26 ft. 3 in. (8 m)
Width	10 ft. 6 in. (3.2 m)
Height	11 ft. 6 in. (3.50 m)
Engine	2 Daimler "165204", 4-cylinder, water-cooled, 100 h.p. each, 800–900 r.p.m.
Speed	6 m.p.h. (9 km.p.h.)
Tank capacity . .	158.4 U.S. gal., 132 Imp. gal. (600 l)
Range	50 miles (80 km)
Armament . . .	1 57-mm Sokol cannon, 6 Maxim mg or 7 Spandau mg
Ammunition . .	500 57-mm rds, 18,000 rds mg
Armor	30 mm
Crew	18
Number in series .	About 20
Year	1917–18

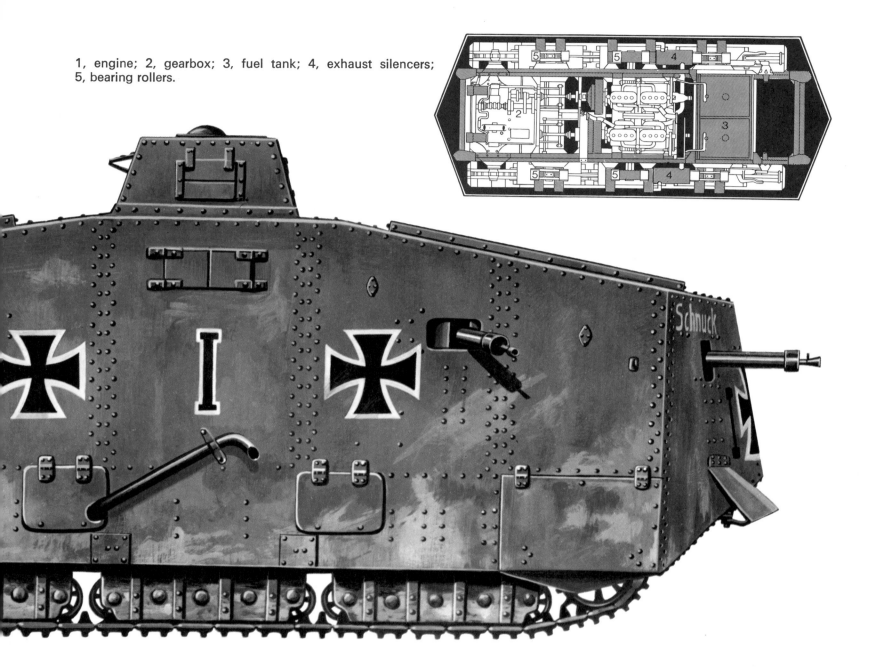

1, engine; 2, gearbox; 3, fuel tank; 4, exhaust silencers;
5, bearing rollers.

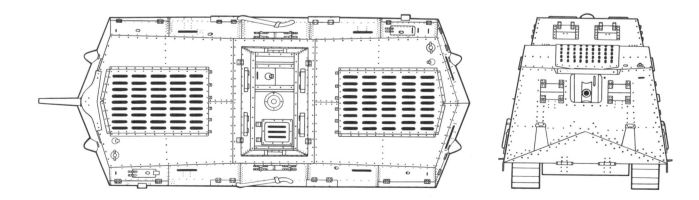

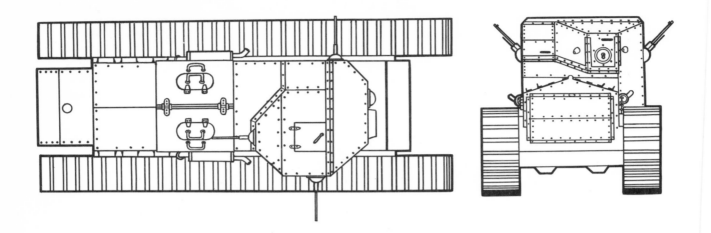

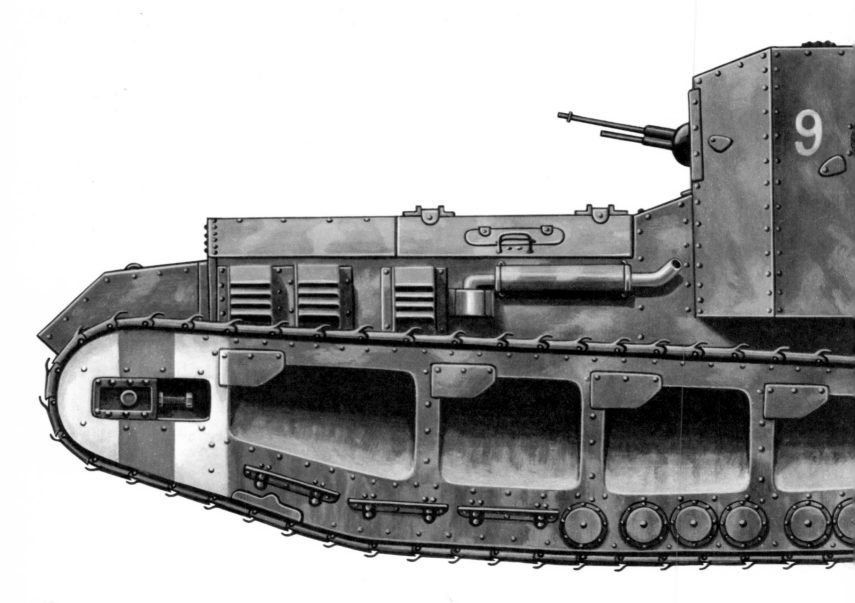

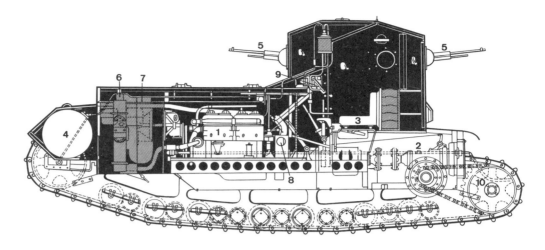

1, engine; 2, gearbox; 3, driver's seat; 4, fuel tank; 5, machine gun; 6, radiator; 7, fan; 8, flywheel; 9, steering wheel; 10, driving wheel.

The "Whippet" Mark A was the first medium tank to enter action in World War I. Like its successors Mark B and Mark C, which were subsequently heavier, it was the first tank with an apparently separate turret. This means that it already displayed the classic silhouette, with track, chassis or hull and gun turret, that still characterizes present-day tanks. How fast the Whippet could get going is proved by an episode in 1918; seven Whippets overran three German battalions entrenched in the south of Villers-Cotteret. That made the tacticians look up and take an interest in the medium tank.

Tank, Medium Mark A "Whippet" (Great Britain)

Weight	15.7 short tons, 14 long tons (14.3 tons)
Length	20 ft. (6.1 m)
Width	8 ft. 7 in. (2.61 m)
Height	9 ft. (2.74 m)
Engine	Tylor, 2 4-cylinder, watercooled, each 45 h.p., 1,250 r.p.m.
Speed	8 m.p.h. (13 km.p.h.)
Tank capacity	84.5 U.S. gal., 70 Imp. gal. (318.2 l)
Range	80 miles (128 km)
Armament	3 Hotchkiss mg
Ammunition	5,400 mg
Armor	14 mm (max)
Crew	3
Number in series	200
Year	1917–18

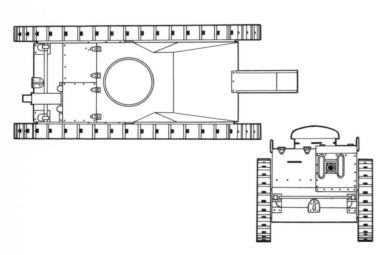

The lightest tank produced so far was made by Ford in 1918. It weighed only three tons and was only 13 ½ feet long and 5 feet 3 inches high. It was manned by a crew of two and the 45-h.p. engine gave it a top speed of about 8 m.p.h. The turret, which did not revolve, was equipped with a single medium machine gun. A steel tail fitted at the rear was to enable the vehicle to traverse even rather wide trenches.

1, driver's seat; 2, engine; 3, machine gun; 4, driving wheels; 5, road wheels; 6, commander's turret; 7, trench-traversing tail.

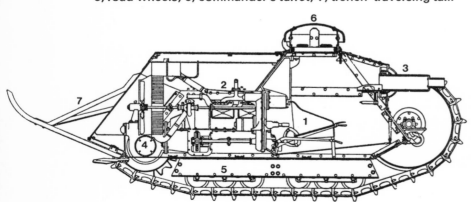

Tank, Ford Two Man   **(U.S.A.)**

Weight	3.4 short tons, 3.05 long tons (3.1 tons)
Length	13 ft. 8 in. (4.15 m)
Width	5 ft. 5 in. (1.65 m)
Height	5 ft. 3 in. (1.6 m)
Engine	2 Ford, 4-cylinder, watercooled, 45 h.p.
Speed	8 m.p.h. (13 km.p.h.)
Tank capacity .	17 U.S. gal., 14.1 Imp. gal. (64.4 l)
Range	34 miles (55 km)
Armament . . .	1 mg
Armor	6.3 mm
Crew	2
Number in series .	15,015 ordered, but by the end of the war only 15 had been produced
Year	1918

Rupprecht Army Group says: "Even if infantrymen can do very little against tanks, yet they must be convinced that they can hold their ground in the face of approaching tanks knowing that the artillery will very soon relieve them of the danger that threatens."

Given this rather light-hearted view of the situation, it is no wonder that the first important tank battle, which started near the small town of Cambrai in northern France on November 20, 1917, was a victory for the British. The British Tank Corps went in with nine battalions equipped with the more highly developed Mark IV tanks, which weighed 28 tons and were powered by a 105 h.p. Daimler engine that gave them a top speed of four miles an hour. The British employed a total of 370 Mark IVs and about a hundred supporting tanks of an earlier type. The experience gained at the Battle of Cambrai was reflected in the next series. The Mark V brought out in 1918 and later the medium tank Mark A, called the "Whippet", had improved steering gear, a more powerful engine and greater obstacle-traversing capability. The Mark V did without the spring-loaded, tail-mounted guide wheels of the first tanks, which were controlled by cables from inside the machine. Provisionally, they used the steering system that had been tried out on "Mother": to turn the tank, one track was slowed down and the other speeded up.

It was only after Cambrai that the Germans realized the value of the tank and endeavoured—literally at the eleventh hour—to catch up with the enemy and if possible turn the tide of war. They built antitank guns and machine guns of 13-mm calibre and equipped mine throwers with low-trajectory undercarriages in order to strengthen their antitank defenses to the utmost. The first German A7V

(continued on page 68)

The White light armored car built in the United States of America in 1918 was employed chiefly by the French army during the last year of the war.

Armored Car, White   **(U.S.A.)**

Weight	6.6 short tons, 5.9 long tons (6 tons)
Length	18 ft. 4 ½ in. (5.6 m)
Width	7 ft. (2.1 m)
Height	9 ft. 0 ¼ in. (2.75 m)
Engine	4-cylinder, watercooled, 35 h.p.
Tank capacity . .	26.42 U.S. gal., 22 Imp. gal. (100 l)
Speed	28 m.p.h. (45 km.p.h.)
Armament . . .	1 37-mm cannon, 2 mg
Ammunition . .	198 cannon rds, 5,500 mg rds
Armor	8 mm
Crew	4
Year	1918

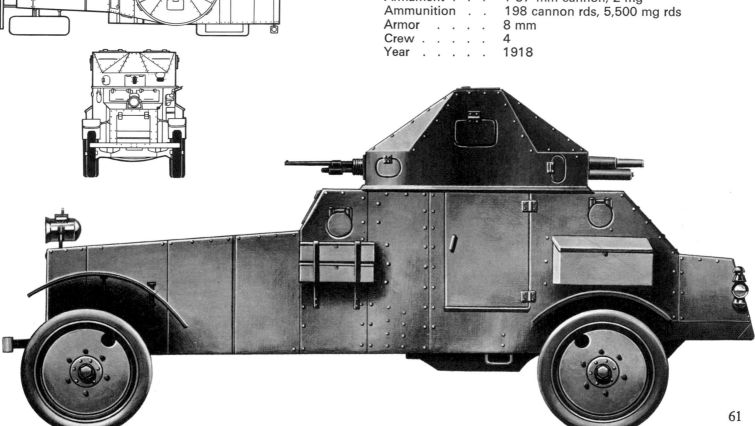

61

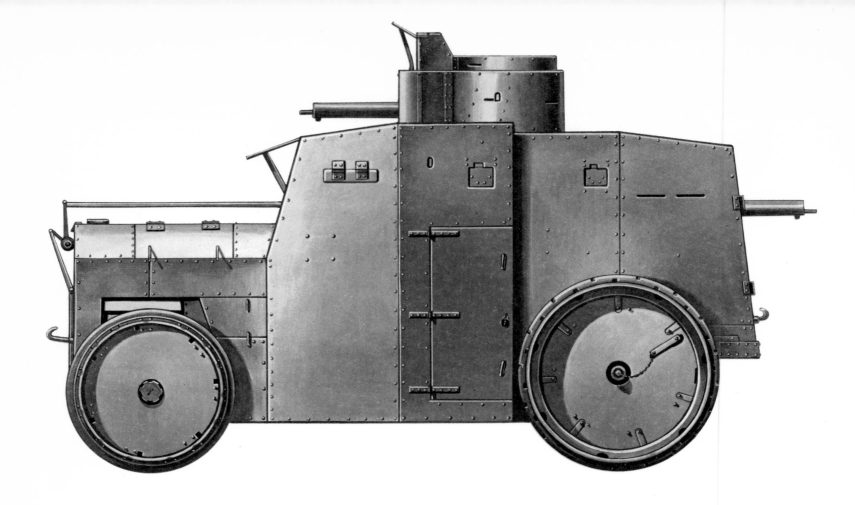

Political considerations dominated the development and construction of the hundred or so armored cars built in Germany by Daimler, Benz and Ehrhardt during the early 1920s. Daimler based theirs on the KD 1 tractor, whereas the other two firms built new, specially designed chassis with front and rear steering. The Interallied Control Commission objected to the rear steering, which was nonetheless adopted and "masked" by a steel plate. Some of these vehicles were put into service as "Schupo-Sonderwagen" (Special Police Cars).

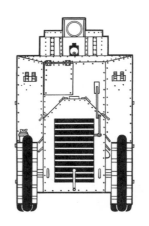

Armored Car, Daimler DZVR or DZR   (Germany)
(Sd. Kfz. 3)

Weight	11.55–13.2 short tons, 10.3–11.8 long tons (10.5–12 tons)
Length	18 ft. 3 ½ in. (5.58 m)
Width	6 ft. 10 ¾ in. (2.1 m)
Height	10 ft. 2 in. (3.1 m)
Engine	Daimler M 1574, 4-cylinder, water-cooled, 100 h.p.
Speed	31 m.p.h. (50 km.p.h.)
Tank capacity . .	52.85 U.S. gal., 44 Imp. gal. (200 l)
Range	186 miles (300 km)
Armament . . .	2 mg
Armor	12 mm, turret 7.5 mm
Crew	6–8
Number in series .	40
Year	1919–20

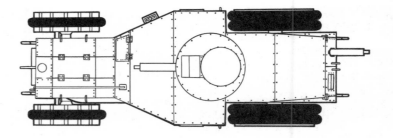

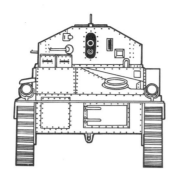

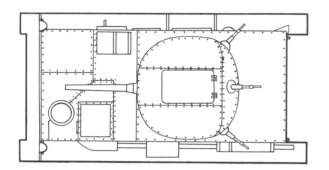

The Vickers Medium Mark II was brought out in England during the interwar period. British tank development at that time was hampered by the tight armament budget and by disagreement among experts as to what role the tank would play in future wars. According to the prevailing theory, it should act like a unit of a fleet at sea, relying on speed and mobility rather than on armor plating for defense against enemy weapons.

Tank, Vickers Medium Mark II   **(Great Britain)**

Weight	14.1 short tons, 12.5 long tons (12.8 tons)
Length	17 ft. 5 ¾ in. (5.32 m)
Width.	9 ft. 1 ½ in. (2.78 m)
Height	8 ft. 10 in. (2.68 m)
Engine	Armstrong Siddeley, 8-cylinder, aircooled, 90 h.p., 1,800 r.p.m.
Speed.	15 m.p.h. (24 km.p.h.)
Tank capacity . .	101.9 U.S. gal., 85 Imp. gal. (386 l)
Range.	119 miles (192 km)
Armament . . .	1 3-pdr (47 mm) QF gun, 6 Vickers mg
Armor	8 mm
Crew	5
Number in series .	160 of MK I and MK II
Year	1923–28

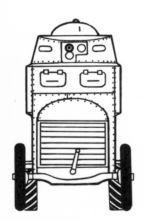

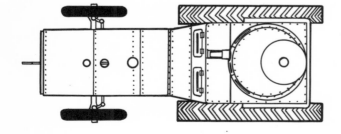

The Citroën-Kégresse M23, a French hybrid, was one of the first armored half-tracks.

Armored Car, Citroën-Kégresse M23   **(France)**
(Autochenille de Cavalerie)

Weight	2.4 short tons, 2.1 long tons (2.2 tons)
Length	10 ft. 9 in. (3.33 m)
Width	4 ft. 5 in. (1.37 m)
Height	7 ft. 4 in. (2.26 m)
Engine	Citroën, 18 h.p.
Speed	25 m.p.h. (40 km.p.h.) (reverse 3.7 m.p.h., 6 km.p.h.)
Tank capacity . .	15.8 U.S. gal., 13.2 Imp. gal. (60 l)
Range	125 miles (200 km)
Armament . . .	1 37-mm cannon or 1 mg
Armor	6 mm
Crew	3
Year	1923–28

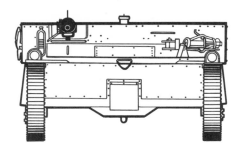

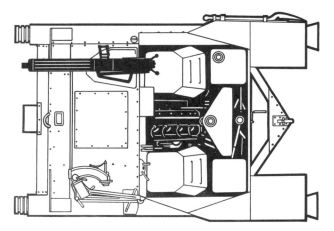

The British Carden-Loyd "tankettes" were mini-tanks with a crew of one or two. They appeared in the early 1930s and were first employed in the Chaco War of 1932–3 between Bolivia and Paraguay. They also took part in the Italo-Abyssinian War and in the Spanish Civil War as machine-gun carriers, mortar carriers, reconnaissance and transport vehicles, and as tractors for antitank guns. They were powered by a 22-h.p. engine and could do about 30 m.p.h. on the road. Their performance in the open country was not very reliable, particularly where vertical obstacles over 16 inches high were encountered.

Light Tank, Carden-Loyd Mark VI　　(Great Britain)

Weight	1.7 short tons, 1.5 long tons (1.6 tons)
Length	8 ft. 1 in. (2.47 m)
Width	5 ft. 7 in. (1.7 m)
Height	4 ft. (1.22 m)
Engine	Ford Model T, 4-cylinder, watercooled, 22 h.p.
Speed	28–30 m.p.h. (45–48 km.p.h.)
Tank capacity . .	12 U.S. gal., 10 Imp. gal. (45.5 l)
Range	100 miles (160 km)
Armament . . .	1 Vickers 303 R.C. Class "C" water-cooled mg
Ammunition . .	1,000 mg rds
Armor	9 mm
Crew	2
Number in series .	Produced in large numbers
Year	1928

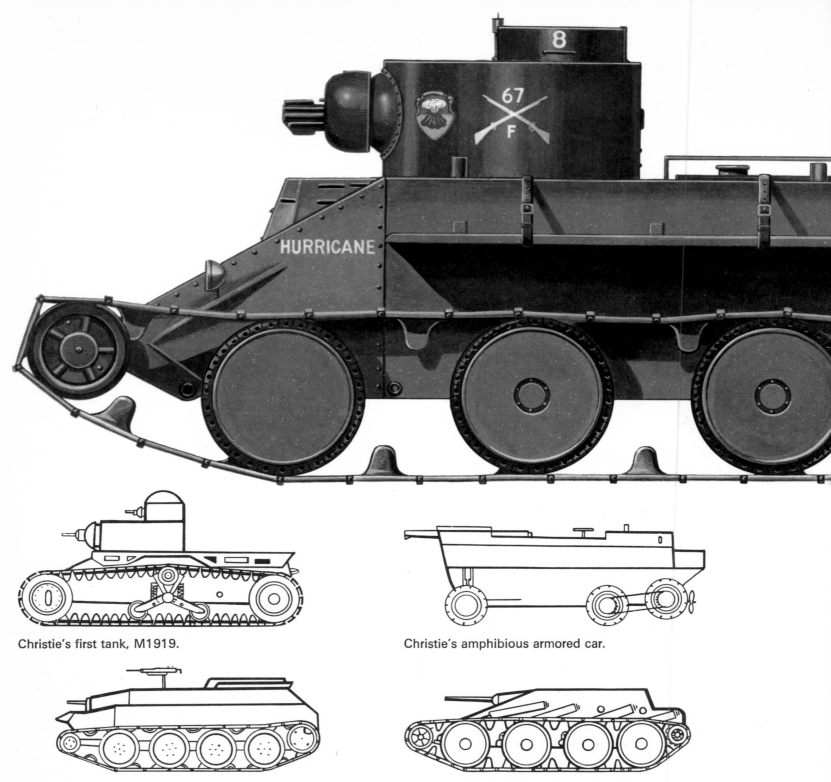

HURRICANE

Christie's first tank, M1919.

Christie's amphibious armored car.

Prototype of 8-ton M1928 tank.

Christie's M1932 tank, precursor of the Crusader.

The M1933 airborne armored car.

Christie's first airborne tank, the M1936.

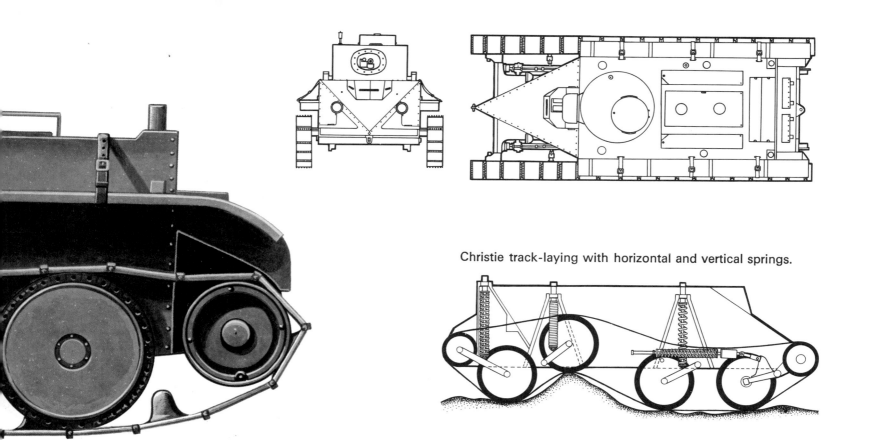

Christie track-laying with horizontal and vertical springs.

Tank, T3 (Christie)   (U.S.A.)

Weight	11.1 short tons, 9.94 long tons (10.1 tons)
Length	18 ft. (5.49 m)
Width	7 ft. 4 in. (2.23 m)
Height	7 ft. 6 in. (2.28 m)
Engine	Ordnance Liberty, 12-cylinder, water-cooled, 338 h.p., 1,400 r.p.m.
Speed	47 m.p.h. without tracks (75 km.p.h.) 27 m.p.h. with tracks (44 km.p.h.)
Tank capacity	89 U.S. gal., 74.1 Imp. gal. (337.3 l)
Range	150 miles (241 km)
Armament	1 37-mm cannon, 1 mg
Ammunition	126 37-mm rds, 3,000 mg rds
Armor	12.7 mm
Crew	3
Number in series	9
Year	1931

During the 1930s J. Walter Christie, the American tank maker, had far and away the best ideas in that field. In his own country they met with a very cool welcome, but some features of his design were incorporated in the Russian BT tank and particularly in the T34 and its successors, which were perhaps the most successful tanks in military history. Christie's decisive contribution was the elimination of the sprockets, so that the track was driven directly by the road wheels. The first Christie Type T3 tank could travel on its solid rubber tires when the tracks were removed; it had no rivals as regards road speed. But the Christie track drive was also a great improvement, as is demonstrated by the fact that the experimental M1937 powered by a 430-h.p. engine did over 46 m.p.h. across country. Christie succeeded in building only nine of his T3 tanks in America. Two of them went to Russia and it was only during World War II that his countrymen realized the value of what they had thrown away a decade before. The British put Christie's ideas to better use and his designs formed the basis of the famous "Crusader" tanks that were produced in 1939 and that gave such good results in the second world war. Christie was also the first to plan light-weight tanks that could be parachuted from aircraft.

tank took the field in 1918. But what chance was there of winning a decisive victory with fifteen tanks made in Germany and thirty captured from the British? Tank met tank for the first time at Villers-Bretonneux on April 24, 1918, and too late the Germans realized that the best way to fight a tank is with another tank—a principle still valid today. There is no question of World War I having been decided by the tank. But it was the first war in history in which technological and economic factors played a preponderant role. The veritable revolution in the art of war began with the appearance on the battlefield of tanks and other motor-vehicles. Thus the importance of an industrial technology and economic power on the outcome of a war was clear to see.

It is true that the tank was not "exploited" to the full in World War I despite Colonel Swinton and other early tank corps officers, who from the start had wanted them to be used in massed formation. But whatever may have been the shortcomings on the part of the Allies, the tank owed much of its remarkable success to its underestimation by the Germans.

The plans and programs for tank construction drawn up by the belligerent Powers speak a very clear language. In 1919 Britain was to have increased its tank fleet by 2,000 to a total of 7,000. The French wanted to have 8,000–10,000 in place of less than 3,000. The United States had had the intention of building 10,000. When the war ended Germany possessed only 45 tanks, including captures, but had planned to have a total of 800 the following year. However the war was lost before the number of tanks planned removed all possible doubts.

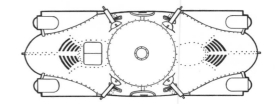

The Skoda P.A.2 tank made a great impression in the 1930s. In fact, the Czech "steel tortoise" not only had the silhouette that later became the rule: with its 85-h.p. engine it could do almost 40 m.p.h. both forwards and in reverse. The Czech manufacturers, particularly Tatra and Skoda, produced technically excellent combat vehicles. During the war the German army profited by the experience of the Czech armament makers. The fast "Hetzer" (Chaser) pursuit tank was based on a Czech model.

Armored Car, Skoda P.A.2   (Czechoslovakia)

Weight	7.7 short tons, 6.9 long tons (7 tons)
Length	20 ft. 4 in. (6.2 m)
Width	7. ft. 2 ¾ in. (2.2 m)
Height	8 ft. 6 ½ in. (2.6 m)
Engine	85 h.p.
Speed	37 m.p.h. forwards and backwards (60 km.p.h.)
Tank capacity	18.49 U.S. gal., 15.39 Imp. gal. (70 l)
Armament	4 mg
Armor	8 mm
Crew	5
Number in series	2
Year	1923–30

Tank, Renault M 1935, R   (France)

Weight	10.8 short tons, 9.7 long tons (9.9 tons)
Length	13 ft. 1 ½ in. (4 m)
Width	6 ft. 0 ¾ in. (1.85 m)
Height	6 ft. 10 ½ in. (2.1 m)
Engine	Renault, 4-cylinder, watercooled, 82 h.p., 2,200 r.p.m.
Speed	12 m.p.h. (19 km.p.h.)
Tank capacity . .	45 U.S. gal., 37.5 Imp. gal. (170.5 l)
Range	50–86 miles (80–138 km)
Armament . . .	1 37-mm cannon SA18, 1 mg
Ammunition . .	58 37-mm rds, 2,500 mg rds
Armor	45 mm
Crew	2
Number in series .	About 2,000
Year	1935–40

At the outbreak of World War II the French army could count on a large number of Renault R35 light tanks. But though weighing only 10 tons, they were too heavy for their 82-h.p. engine; this made them awkward for cross-country operation. The two-man crew also complained of bad visibility. The R35 was interesting for its suspension.

The light Renault M 1935 R was the chief weapon of the French army. By 1940 some 2000 tanks of this type had come off the assembly lines.

The Wheel Suspension of the Renault R35
1, rubber spring;
2, oscillating arm;
3, limiting device;
4, wheel.

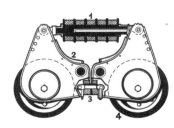

Tank, B-1 BIS   **(France)**

Weight	34.6 short tons, 31 long tons (31.5 tons)
Length	20 ft. 11 in. (6.98 m)
Width	8 ft. 2 in. (2.49 m)
Height	9 ft. 2 in. (2.79 m)
Engine	Renault, 6-cylinder, watercooled, 307 h.p.
Speed	18 m.p.h. (29 km.p.h.)
Range	130 miles (209 km)
Armament . . .	1 75-mm cannon, 1 47-mm cannon, 2 mg
Armor	20–60 mm
Crew	4
Number in series .	About 500
Year	1940

The French Renault B-1 BIS incorporated some important innovations. The 3-ton vehicle afforded its 4-man crew excellent visibility in all directions when the turret hatch was closed; it also had an emergency exit in the floor. The wheels were protected against light artillery fire by lateral steel plates. This vehicle saw little action in the field and so could not show what it was really worth. The Americans found ideas in it for their M3 and the British for the Churchill.

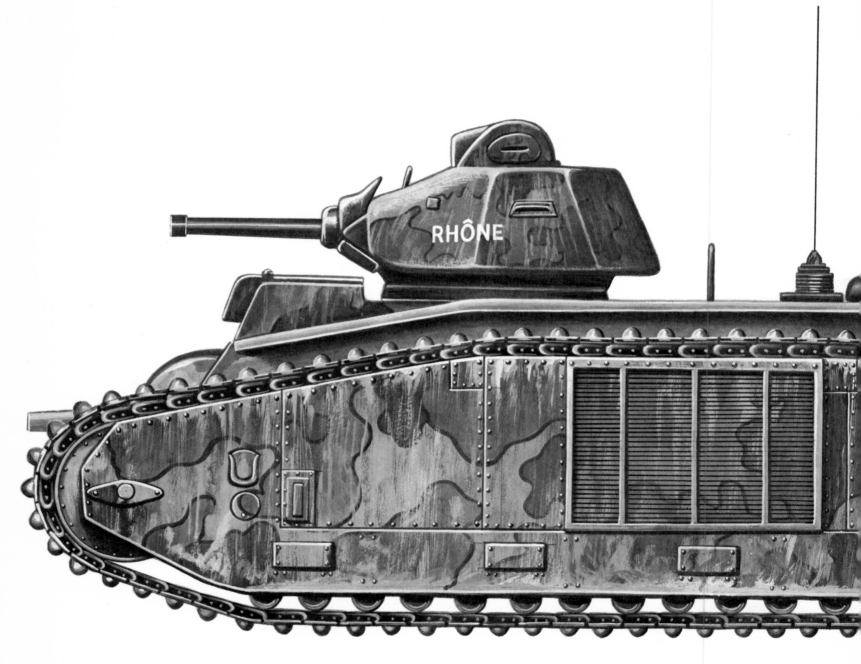

"Aim at the hatches!" was the motto of the German anti-tank gunners who engaged the French B-1 BIS, a heavy combat vehicle with little mobility but strong armor plating.

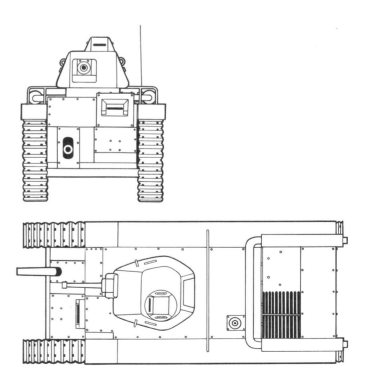

The French Somua S 35 was greatly admired by the German armored troops during the French campaign of 1940. It was a cavalry tank weighing nearly 20 tons and capable of about 25 m.p.h. on the road. An excellent system of telescopes afforded the three-man crew adequate visibility. The turret was cast in one piece 1 ½ inches thick.

The French 3C was the heaviest tank of the C series, a limited number of which were supplied to the French army in the late 1920s. It was designed as a breakthrough tank but had so little mobility that it was a death-trap for the crew. Even more exaggerated were Velpry's plans for a 600-ton tank that never got beyond the drawing-board stage.

Tank, Somua S 35 (France)

Weight	22.1 short tons, 19.7 long tons (20 tons)
Length	17 ft. 4 in. (5.3 m)
Width	6 ft. 11 in. (2.12 m)
Height	8 ft. 6 in. (2.62 m)
Engine	Somua, 8-cylinder, watercooled, 190 h.p., 2,000 r.p.m.
Speed	25 m.p.h. (40 km.p.h.)
Tank capacity .	109 U.S. gal., 90.8 Imp. gal. (413 l)
Range	80–161 miles (129–260 km)
Armament . . .	1 47-mm cannon SA 35, 1 mg
Ammunition . .	118 47-mm rds, 1,250 mg rds
Armor	55 mm
Crew	3
Number in series .	About 500
Year	1935–40

Heavy Tank, 3C (France)

Weight	78.1 short tons, 70 long tons (71 tons)
Length	39 ft. 4 ¼ in. (12 m)
Width	9 ft. 7 in. (2.92 m)
Height	13 ft. 3 in. (4.04 m)
Engine	3 engines each of 660 h.p.
Speed	8 m.p.h. (13 km.p.h.)
Tank capacity .	396.35 U.S. gal., 330.3 Imp. gal. (1,500 l)
Range	74–93 miles (120–150 km)
Armament . . .	1 155-mm Howitzer, 1 75-mm cannon, 2 mg, 4 reserve mg
Ammunition . .	About 150 cannon rds, about 5,000 mg rds
Armor	50 mm, turret 35 mm
Crew	13
Year	1924–26

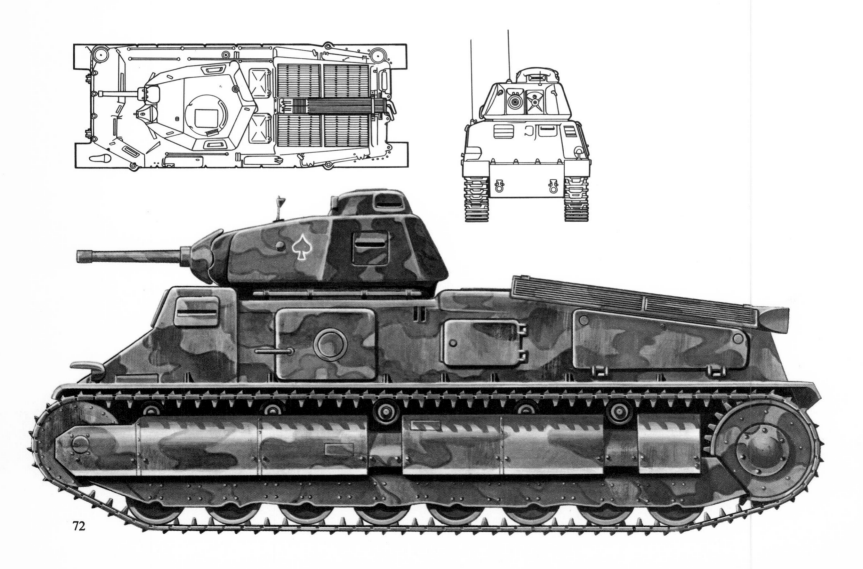

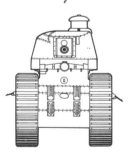

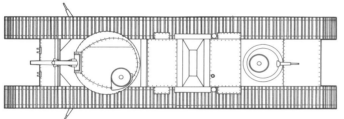

Here, stuck in the mud, is one of the French 2C supertanks that saw action at the outbreak of World War II, twenty years after they were built. Their 70 tons soon proved their doom.

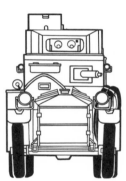

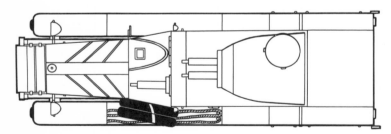

**Armored Car, Lanchester Mark I, (Great Britain)
IA, II and IIA**

Weight	7.4 short tons, 6.6 long tons (6.75 tons) Mark I–IA
	8.2 short tons, 7.4 long tons (7.45 tons) Mark II–IIA
Length	20 ft. (6.09 m)
Width	6 ft. 7 ½ in. (1.96 m)
Height	9 ft. 3 in. (3 m)
Engine	Lanchester, 6-cylinder, watercooled, 40–60 h.p., 2,000 r.p.m.
Speed	45 m.p.h. (72 km.p.h.)
Tank capacity . .	26.42 U.S. gal., 22 Imp. gal. (100 l)
Range	200 miles (320 km)
Armament . . .	1 Vickers mg 0.5 in., 2 Vickers mg 0.303 in.
Ammunition . .	1,000 mg–0.5 in. rds, 5,000 mg–7.7-mm rds
Armor	6–9 mm
Crew	4
Number in series .	39
Year	1931

A large number of Lanchester armored cars, of which there were various versions, were commissioned for the British ground forces. This was the first combat vehicle to have a chassis specially designed for the purpose. The four rear wheels were driven, which gave the Lanchester a far greater cross-country capability than other machines of its type. In 1940 a Lanchester armored car was specially converted and fitted out for a less bellicose use—to carry cabinet ministers and other V.I.P.s.

74

World War II   4

Almost ever since it was sent into action at Cambrai in 1917 the tank has been the major subject of expert military debate. No wonder the part it played in World War II is the focal point of these disputes, which are at times very heated. It is undoubtedly right to say—and a great many historians agree in this—that World War II was a tank war. Certainly not in the sense that tanks used singly or reduced to the role of infantry support weapons decided the issue, but as a war of large mechanized units that could count on weapons of every sort, the most important of which was the tank. One must not, however, over-estimate the scope of earthbound weapons: the tank could never have played the decisive role it did were it not for the presence of the air force.

Some people speak of tanks and aircraft as if they were twin weapons which both in co-operation and in bitter opposition prepared and decided the issue of the war. Within the framework of their unholy relationship their indirect confrontation counted more than direct contact between land and air. It is true that tank units could only operate unmolested when mastery of the air was assured. It is also true that air forces can boast some successes over armored units. But where aircraft won the most decisive victories over tanks was when the latter were attacked before they could travel a mile or fire a shot—bombing them on the assembly lines of the belligerent countries' industrial centres.

After the war British military experts wrote sarcastically that Britain lost her tank battles in the offices and on the desks of Imperial General Staff and of the Army Research Board. As a matter of fact, the foundations of Germany's amazing success with tanks in World War II were laid immediately after the end of World War I. While the Germans drew the correct conclusions from that catastrophe, the British and French tacticians made the wrong decisions that were fraught with such fatal results. A British officer on the Allied Control Commission, who had the task of supervising the destruction of the German tanks, told his German opposite number at the time that they were lucky to be rid of their old machines and so have the opportunity one day of making a fresh start with something newer and better.

The Treaty of Versailles imposed severe restrictions on the equipment of the German army. But Britain too abandoned the speedy development of her own range of tanks, which were in the lead at that time. In the winter of 1918 the War Ministry decided to discontinue tank production and suspend work on projects in hand. Only medium Marks C and D were still to be built, but the Treasury refused to release the funds for the Mark C, with the result that the 450 machines already under construction were never finished. Only a single prototype of the Mark D was built and tried out successfully in the Midlands during the following summer. It had a top speed of almost 20 miles an hour, which made it four times as fast as the machines employed during the war. Not long after that the British army took delivery of the first Vickers tanks, but their performance was not up to the best technical level of the day.

The French military authorities also neglected their tanks, which included the relatively handy Renaults that could have been developed into a very useful strike force. After the war General Estienne, who had drawn the correct conclusions as to the value of mechanization for

(continued on page 78)

When the limitations imposed on German tank development were dropped in 1933, the military authorities called for a rather light tank that would involve a less costly training program. Taking their cue from the British Carden-Loyd, Krupp built 150 light tanks, which were supplied to the army under the name "P I" Model A. More of them were commissioned until finally there were enough to equip the first three German tank divisions. Some saw action in the Spanish Civil War. Subsequently, when more sophisticated models were available, the German army fitted out some as tank destroyers and equipped others as command tanks for squadron leaders.

In his "Panzerführer" (Tank Commander), General Guderian sets forth some of the reasons that led to the construction of the P II tank. He says that the appearance of the more efficient P III and P IV was delayed. This led the High Command to decide on the P II as a stop-gap. Its manufacture was entrusted to the MAN (Maschinenfabrik Augsburg-Nürnberg) company and production got under way in the mid-1930s. Several models, each an improvement on its predecessor, were built and delivered. In the French campaign of 1940 the German army had 955 tanks of this type. According to plan, 1,067 P IIs were to have come off the assembly lines in 1941, but in the event the number was reduced to 860. The P II was slightly inferior to the Russian tanks and did not stand up too well to the latest antitank weapons. Though originally designed for training purposes, the P II performed extraordinarily well in the field. One specimen of Model F is still extant: it was captured by the British in North Africa and is now on view in the Tank Museum at Bovington.

PzKpfw II, Ausführung F (Sd.Kfz. 121)   (Germany)

Weight	10.4 short tons, 9.3 long tons (9.5 tons)
Length	15 ft. 3 in. (4.81 m)
Width	7 ft. 4 in. (2.28 m)
Height	6 ft. 6 in. (2.02 m)
Engine	Maybach HL 62 TR, 6-cylinder, water-cooled, 140 h.p., 2,600 r.p.m.
Speed	25 m.p.h. (40 km.p.h.)
Tank capacity . .	44.9 U.S. gal., 37.4 Imp. gal. (170 l)
Range	77–118 miles (125–175 km)
Armament . . .	1 20-mm KwK 30 or KwK 38, 1 mg
Ammunition . .	180 20-mm rds, 2,550 mg rds
Armor	35 mm, turret 30 mm
Crew	3
Number in series .	650
Year	1940–44

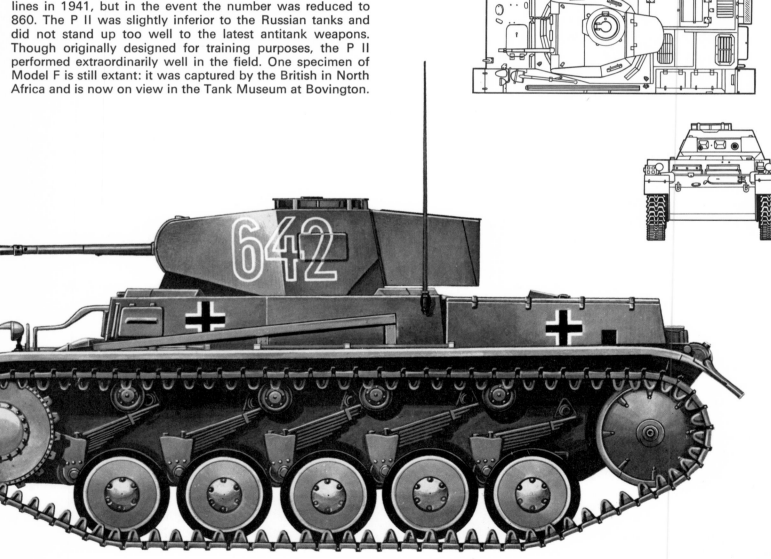

The PI tank was standard equipment in the German army.

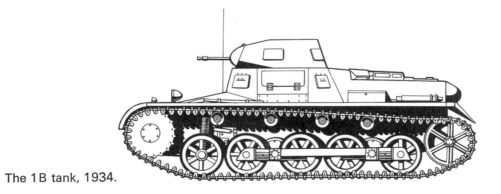

The 1B tank, 1934.

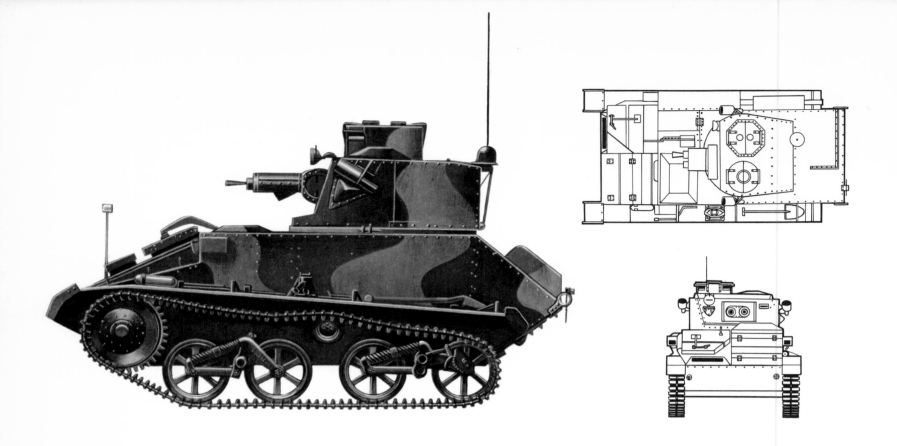

Tank, Mark VIA   (Great Britain)

Weight	5.7 short tons, 5.1 long tons (5.2 tons)
Length	13 ft. 2 in. (4.01 m)
Width	6 ft. 10 in. (2.08 m)
Height	7 ft. 5 in. (2.26 m)
Engine	Meadows, 6-cylinder, 88 h.p., 2,800 r.p.m.
Speed	35 m.p.h. (56 km.p.h.)
Range	131 miles (211 km)
Armament . . .	1 mg, 2 smoke dischargers
Ammunition . .	2,900 rds mg
Armor	14 mm
Crew	3
Number in series .	Over a thousand of all models in this light tank series
Year	1937–39

The light British Mark IV of the Vickers Carden-Loyd series was constantly improved. The Mark VIA was delivered to the army in 1938. At the outbreak of hostilities the British ground forces had some thousand of these vehicles in addition to 146 heavier tanks. Technically, the Vickers Carden-Loyd was a well developed tank and did yeoman duty as a reconnaissance machine in every British theatre of war.

land forces, demanded that tanks should operate on their own and in so doing voiced a criticism of the army's traditional, hidebound ideas. He was the first French soldier to insist that tanks should be used on missions of strategic importance. In the 1930s General Charles de Gaulle, then still a Colonel, adopted Estienne's views and developed his own novel ideas on how a war should be fought. The visionary lecture delivered by Colonel Joseph Doumenc at the Centre des Hautes Etudes Militaires in summer 1927 is very interesting. This is what he said: "Mobilization has been decided for X Day at 00.00 hours. Six hours

later the tank corps, which is stationed in the Bordeaux region, is already on the Seine. At 10.00 hours it reaches the Eastern frontier." He went on to describe the inevitable annihilation of the enemy forces by the advancing tank units and concluded with the remark that such were the prospects for tomorrow.

But, like their opposite numbers in Britain, most French army men did not agree with the ideas of their more progressive colleagues. The *Instruction sur l'Emploi des Chars de Combat* (Directive on the Use of Tanks) says: "Tanks are infantry escort weapons which in an emergency are attached singly or in groups to certain large formations. In battle tanks, whether singly or in groups, act within the framework of the infantry. Tanks are merely support weapons, which may be assigned to the infantry for a limited time; they considerably augment its striking force but do not replace it." The document goes on to state very clearly that the tank must be subordinated to the infantry. "Tanks can neither take the place of infantry nor increase its combat value, because their efficiency in battle is too greatly curtailed. Consequently, co-operation between tanks and infantry must be regulated by narrowly limited and permanently valid rules. But the most reliable way to ensure this is to place the tank units under the orders of the commanding officers of the most advanced infantry forces in a given section of the front."

This shows that the situation at that time was characterized by a struggle between diametrically opposed theories as to the best method of using tanks. In Britain there was, as a rule, greater support for the idea of throwing them into action suddenly and in large numbers, though there too some people wanted to brand the tank as nothing more than an auxiliary weapon for the infantry. In Germany Guderian summed up the situation: "Do we want to destine tank troops for close co-operation with the infantry or to use them for enveloping and outflanking operations in the open field? Do we want, if we are forced into a defensive war, to seek a rapid decision on the ground by large-scale, co-ordinated employment of the major striking force, or do we want to forgo its inherent capacity for fast, long-range movement, chain it to the slow tempo of infantry and artillery warfare and so abandon from the start all hope of achieving a rapid decision of the battle and the war?"

Once Guderian had defined the tank as the one and only decisive weapon, the success of the German armored troops was an absolute certainty. But that does not mean that his views were accepted without opposition. Even a so highly respected tank expert found it difficult to persuade the German armed forces to translate his plans into action. The German High Command, and particularly General Beck, Chief of the General Staff, were extraordinarily sceptical towards Guderian's plans and at the start were chary of overestimating the value of the tank as a weapon and employing it in large-scale operations in depth. One of their arguments was that in other countries no examples of this use of armor had been observed. It was Guderian who coined the term that proved so true in the course of World War II—to Germany's discomfiture, in the long run—he called armored troops the "architects of victory".

The Russian theoreticians had excellent ideas as to how tanks should be employed, but they dissipated the strength of their armored units by providing fast tanks for break-through action, heavy tanks for defensive action and light tanks as infantry support weapons. In line with the "all tank action" theory—developed in Britain but not consistently applied in practice there—which involved the wholesale employment of large tank units, the Soviet Union formulated a doctrine on tank warfare based on achieving a breakthrough into the depths of the enemy territory. The objectives were artillery positions, command headquarters, general staffs, supply depots and reserves, in fact, all the essential rear echelons. The "Red Worker and Peasant Army Active Service Order" of 1936 says: "Modern combat weapons, chiefly tanks, artillery, aircraft and mechanized units, employed on a large scale, offer the possibility of launching attacks against the entire depth of the enemy formation simultaneously, the objective being to cut off, encircle and destroy the enemy troops." Another passage of the Order deals with the duties of what are termed "long-range tank units": "Long-range tank units have the task of breaking through to the rear of the defender's main forces in order to smash their reserves and staffs, annihilate their major artillery units, and cut off the retreat of the main enemy forces."

Before the outbreak of the second world war no armed forces in any country had the slightest experience of the leadership and maintenance of large mechanized units. Consequently no one could foresee how the new weapon would stand up to actual combat conditions. When the Germans launched their surprise attack on Poland in 1939 the Poles had 36 infantry divisions, 11 cavalry brigades and one mountain brigade. They also had two tank brigades with a total of some 500 armored vehicles, most of which, however, dated from World War I or shortly after. They were completely lacking in effective antitank weapons and their air-force and anti-aircraft defences were quite inadequate. Though their armor was relatively strong, there was not a single direct encounter between their tanks and the Germans' during the four weeks that the campaign lasted. Nonetheless, that campaign was a sort of trial by fire for armored troops and a turning point in the history of war. It was all over inside four weeks, and the outcome was largely ascribed to the German armor which, in combination with the vastly superior German air arm, was responsible for the decisive thrust. Guderian's views on the use of tanks, which had until then been shared by very few military experts on the international level, were proved to be correct. It was only when they were sent into action independently of the infantry as self-contained units that tanks succeeded in launching decisive attacks. It was further found that where tank units were concerned all other arms—artillery, sappers, even service troops—had to be treated as auxiliaries and given adequate speed and

(continued on page 91)

To make good the weak points of the Mark I infantry tank, which was slow and carried only a single machine gun, the British army commissioned the "Matilda" Mark II from Vickers, who passed the order on to the Vulcan Foundry Company. Even before Dunkirk, the "Matilda" was a tough proposition for the German tank troops: it stood up to all antitank weapons available at that time. "Matildas" fought in North Africa and some were supplied to the Red Army for training purposes.

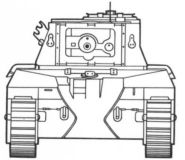

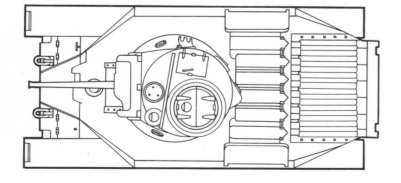

Infantry Tank, A.12 Mark IIA,   **(Great Britain)**
Matilda III

Weight	29.7 short tons, 26.5 long tons (27 tons)
Length	18 ft. 5 in. (5.61 m)
Width	8 ft. 6 in. (2.59 m)
Height	8 ft. 3 in. (2.52 m)
Engine	2 Leyland E 148 and E 149 or E 164 and E 165, 6-cylinder, watercooled, 95 h.p., 2,000 r.p.m.
Speed	15 m.p.h. (24 km.p.h.)
Tank capacity . .	55.8 U.S. gal., 46.5 Imp. gal. (211.4 l)
Range	80 (cross-country)–160 (road) miles (128–257 km)
Armament . . .	1 Mark IX or X, 2-pounder QF, 1 mg 2 smoke dischargers, 1 light mg
Ammunition . .	93 2 pdr rds, 2,925 mg rds, 600 light mg rds
Armor	78 mm, turret 70 mm
Crew	4
Number in series .	2,987 of all marks
Year	1939–42

The Italian M13/40, though originally designed as a pursuit tank, became the chief weapon of the Italian armored troops in North Africa. The plan was to replace this small vehicle, which though not very fast gave a good account of itself, with the German P III built under licence in Italy. Owing to delay on the part of the German government, the Italians decided to continue building their own light tank, which suffered heavy losses on the North African front. During an engagement near El Alamein, 17 of the 19 Italian tanks were destroyed.

Medium Tank, M13/40 (Italy)

Weight	15.4 short tons, 13.7 long tons (14 tons)
Length	16 ft. 2 in. (4.93 m)
Width	7 ft. 4 ½ in. (2.25 m)
Height	7 ft. 10 in. (2.39 m)
Engine	SPA ST Diesel, 8-cylinder, 105 h.p., 1,800 r.p.m.
Speed	20 m.p.h. (32 km.p.h.)
Tank capacity . .	42 U.S. gal., 35 Imp. gal. (159 l)
Range	124 miles (198 km)
Armament . . .	1 47-mm SA gun, 1 mg
Ammunition . .	104 47-mm rds, 3,048 mg rds
Armor	30 mm, turret 42 mm
Number in series .	About 2,000
Year	1940–41

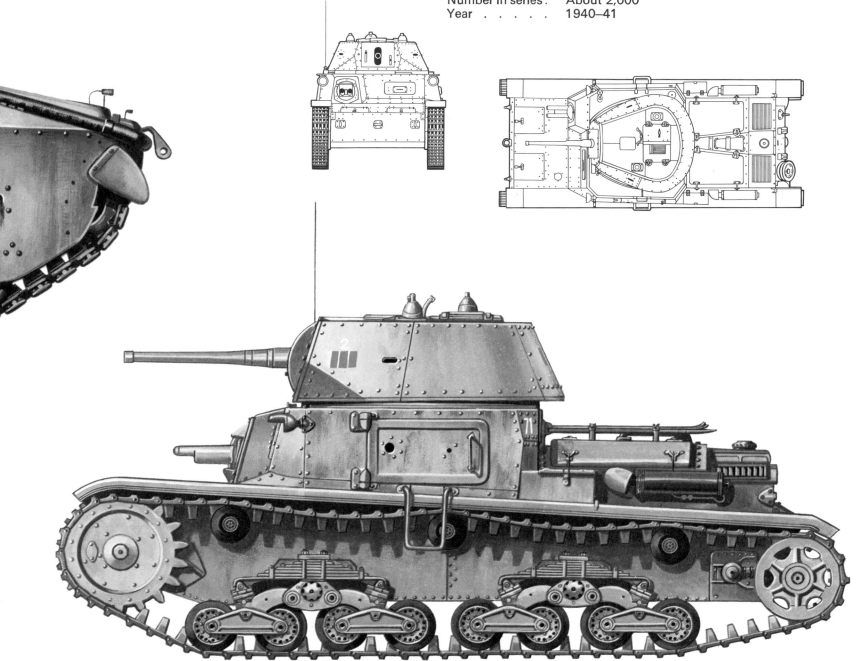

German infantrymen were always glad to get a ride in a
P III tank. In the desert a yard driven was one gained.

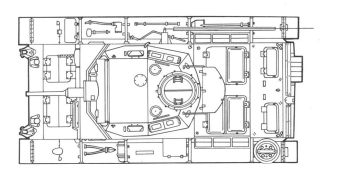

The P III tank was designed to be the German army's chief combat vehicle. But during the "Blitzkrieg" against Poland in September 1939 the actual tank training regiment had only a few tanks of this type. The P III was the first tank to possess the qualities which expert tactician General Guderian had been insisting on for years. When the French campaign started the German army had 349 tanks of this type, and the initial victories in Russia would have been impossible without the lárge number of P IIIs employed there. The choice of the P III's armament was a matter of serious contention. When Hitler discovered that the army had disobeyed his orders and equipped it with a 37 instead of a 50-mm cannon, he flew into a rage and took tank development into his own hands.

PzKpfw III, Ausführung F (Sd. Kfz. 141)   (Germany)

Weight	24.5 short tons, 21.9 long tons (22.3 tons)
Length	17 ft. 9 in. (5.41 m)
Width	9 ft. 7 in. (2.92 m)
Height	8 ft. 3 in. (2.51 m)
Engine	Maybach HL 120 TRm, 12-cylinder, watercooled, 300 h.p., 3,000 r.p.m.
Speed	11–25 m.p.h. (18–40 km.p.h.)
Tank capacity . .	86.4 U.S. gal., 72 Imp. gal. (327 l)
Range	109–160 miles (175–257 km)
Armament . . .	1 50-mm KwK 39 L/60 or 50 mm L/42, 1 mg
Ammunition . .	99 50-mm rds, 2,000 mg rds
Armor	30 mm, turret 30 mm
Crew	5
Number in series .	5,650 of all types
Year	1939–43

Column of P IIIs advancing across the Russian plain.

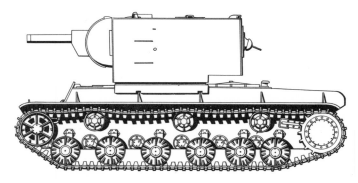

The KV2 with 122-mm or 152-mm howitzer.

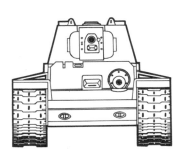

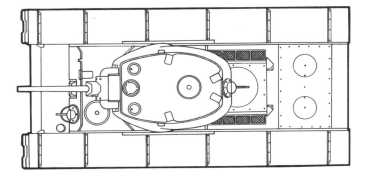

The heavy Russian Klimenti Voroshilov KV1 surprised the Germans when it first appeared in the field. The KV1 and the legendary T34 were the Red Army's chief weapons from 1940 to 1942. The KV1's three-inch armor plating could stand up to the usual antitank guns and even under the most unfavourable conditions the only thing that could stop it was a direct hit from an 88-mm anti-aircraft gun. Its successor the KV2 mounted a 152-mm howitzer in its huge turret.

Heavy Tank, Klimenti Voroshilov KV1A   (U.S.S.R.)

Weight	52 short tons, 46.2 long tons (47 tons)
Length	22 ft. (6.7 m)
Width	10 ft. 8 in. (3.25 m)
Height	9 ft. (2.74 m)
Engine	Diesel, 12-cylinder, 600 h.p., 2,000 r.p.m.
Speed	25 m.p.h. (40 km.p.h.)
Tank capacity . .	159 U.S. gal., 132.5 Imp. gal. (602.6 l)
Range	124–208 miles (199–334 km)
Armament . . .	1 76.2-mm gun, 3 mg
Ammunition . .	111 76.2-mm rds, 3,024 mg rds
Armor	75 mm
Crew	5
Number in series .	Produced in large numbers
Year	1940

Medium Tank, M3 (Lee Mk1)*   **(U.S.A.)**

Weight	31 short tons, 26.9 long tons (27.4 tons)
Length	18 ft. 6 in. (5.64 m)
Width	8 ft. 11 in. (2.79 m)
Height	10 ft. 4 in. (3.15 m)
Engine	Wright R-975-EC2, 9-cylinder, aircooled, 400 h.p., 2,400 r.p.m.
Speed	22 m.p.h. (35 km.p.h.)
Tank capacity . .	174 U.S. gal., 145 Imp. gal. (659 l)
Range	146 miles (235 km)
Armament . . .	1 75-mm M2 gun, 1 37-mm M5 gun, 4 mg
Ammunition . .	41 75-mm rds, 179 37-mm rds, 8,000 mg rds
Armor	50 mm
Crew	6
Number in series .	About 5,000 of all types
Year	1941–42

* British designation in parentheses

The M3 "General Lee", a medium tank built in the United States, was supplied to Britain in large numbers under the lend-lease agreement. A total of some five thousand M3s were built by the American Locomotive Company and two other firms. Equipped with a British turret and rechristened "General Grant", it chalked up great victories when it first appeared on the North African front. Later, however, the monstrous vehicle fell an easy prey to the German 88-mm antitank gun. The M3, though marked "limited standard" by the Americans, was employed in the field until 1944.

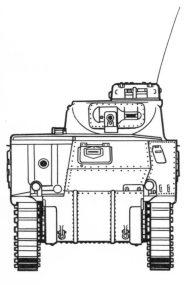

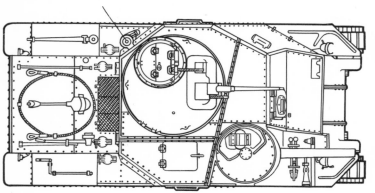

ELH—Egypt's Last Hope—was the Allied troops' name for the American M3. The cross-section shows the typical 9-cylinder radial engine in the stern. All versions could be powered by either Wright or Continental engines.

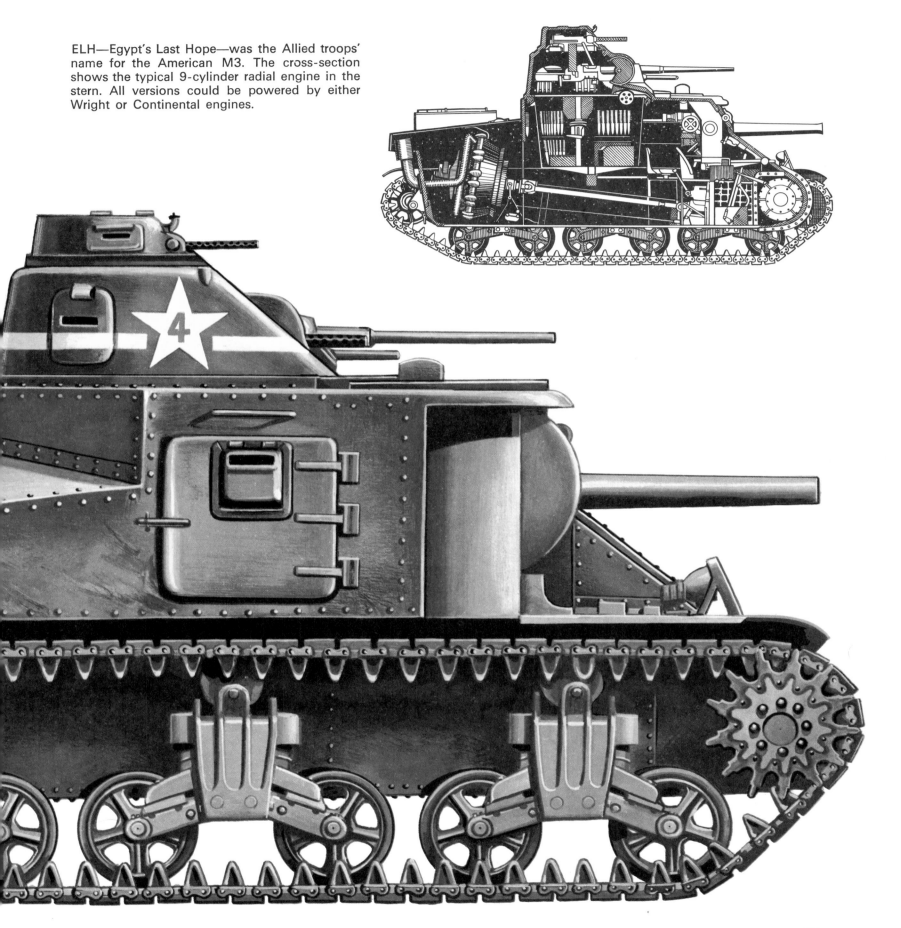

The M3 General Lee in flames.

British Crusader IIs advancing at El Alamein.

In the late 1920s British tank tactitians evolved the concept of cruiser tanks breaking through the front line and penetrating the enemy hinterland. This concept, which was borrowed from the Navy, required the construction of extremely mobile medium tanks. One of these was the Crusader Mark VI. This 20-ton vehicle was the last member of a series originated in the thirties. Employed chiefly in the North African campaign, it also saw action in Europe.

Tank, A.15 Cruiser Mark VI (Great Britain)
Crusader II

Weight	22.1 short tons, 19.7 long tons (20.1 tons)
Length	19 ft. 7 ½ in. (5.99 m)
Width	9 ft. 1 in. (2.77 m)
Height	7 ft. 4 in. (2.24 m)
Engine	Nuffield Liberty Mark III, 12-cylinder, watercooled, 340 h.p., 1,500 r.p.m.
Speed	27 m.p.h. (44 km.p.h.)
Tank capacity	168 U.S. gal., 140 Imp. gal. (637 l)
Range	200 miles (322 km)
Armament	1 40 QF 2-pdr Mark IX or Mark X, 3 mg, 1 smoke discharger
Ammunition	110 cannon rds, 5,100 mg rds, 26 smoke candles
Armor	30—49 mm
Crew	5
Number in series	5,300 Marks I–III
Year	1941

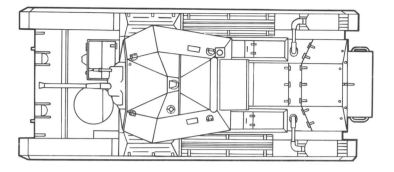

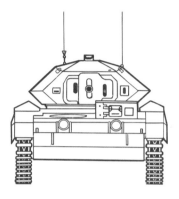

cross-country ability if they were to keep up with the attacks launched by the tanks. It appeared, however, during the Polish campaign, and to some extent right up to the end of the war, that not all military authorities were willing to see things on a large scale. In fact there were many cases where fast armored troops were split up and sometimes even placed under the control of the infantry. This led to time-consuming congestion and to the formation of mixed units which were prevented by differences in speed from operating effectively, with the result that the best chances were thrown away. Even after the Polish campaign German footsoldiers were to sing *Die Infanterie, die Königin der Waffen* (Infantry, Queen of Arms), a song that then expressed the ideas of most military commanders.

If the Polish campaign provided some knowledge of the use of armored troops on the battlefield, it offered little in the way of practical experience. All this changed completely when large numbers of hostile tanks clashed head-on for the first time, namely in the French campaign of 1940. At the outset of what they called the Western Campaign the Germans could count on some 2,500 tanks, of which 450 had been built in Czechoslovakia and equipped with a 37-mm cannon. The majority were PzKw Is and PzKw IIs but there were a few PzKw IIIs, which were also equipped with a 37-mm cannon and some even with a 50-mm cannon. The first PzKw IVs had a 75-mm cannon. At the first encounters between German and Allied tanks it was found that the 37-mm cannon was no use against the heavy armor of the British Matilda. The Germans only gained the upper hand when they were in a position to employ their 88-mm anti-aircraft guns.

France had the strongest army on the European continent and together with Britain had almost twice as many tanks as Germany. Not only were the c. 2,500 German tanks faced with c. 4,800 on the Allied side; the PzKw Is and PzKw IIs were also inferior to their opponents. France had no open flank, such as the German army had found and exploited in Poland. So the German tanks were unable to carry out an enveloping, encircling movement. What is more, the French frontier on the East was hermetically sealed off by the Maginot Line. The French armored divisions with their 175 light and medium tanks were numerically inferior to the corresponding German units but their vehicles were more heavily armored. It was found, however, that tanks did not depend for success on the classic factor of protective armor. In fact, since the German tanks were rather faster and fitted with better radio equipment, they could be used more purposefully and were finally victorious. French tank tactics were unable to cope with the mobile German methods. The inferences drawn from the Polish campaign were confirmed

(continued on page 102)

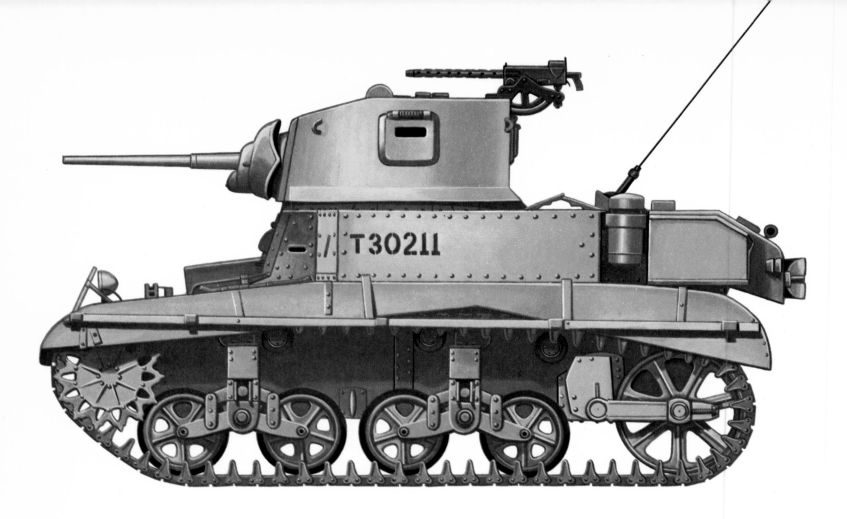

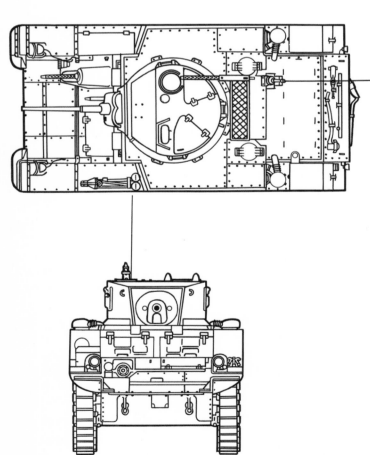

When the first American-built Stuart tanks reached the British forces in North Africa they were the best combat vehicles of that day. It was only when the German tanks were equipped with better cannon and heavier armor that the light Stuarts were limited to the role for which they were originally designed. The Stuart was constantly improved and the Mark III and Mark IV delivered in 1942 already boasted a stabilized cannon which could be fired with a certain degree of accuracy even while the vehicle was in motion.

Light Tank, M3A1 (Stuart III)*   (U.S.A.)

Weight	14.3 short tons, 12.8 long tons (13 tons)
Length	14 ft. 10 in. (4.52 m)
Width	7 ft. 6 in. (2.29 m)
Height	7 ft. 4 in. (2.23 m)
Engine	Continental Model W 670-9A, 7-cylinder, aircooled, 250 h.p., 2,400 r.p.m.
Speed	36 m.p.h. (58 km.p.h.)
Tank capacity . .	56 U.S. gal., 50 Imp. gal. (212 l)
Range	60 miles (96 km)
Armament . . .	1 37-mm M6 L/57, 3 mg
Ammunition . .	111 37-mm rds, 7,000 mg rds
Armor	51 mm
Crew	4
Number in series .	4,621 of all models
Year	1942–43

* British designation in parentheses

The Daimler armored car was commissioned by the British army in 1938 and continued with various improvements well into the 1940s. It weighed rather more than 7 tons and was so popular with the troops that in 1944 one regiment refused to exchange their old Daimlers for brand-new American Staghounds. It kept its vehicles and when the war ended in 1945 handed them over to another unit. Some of those cars were still in service with the territorial army until 1965.

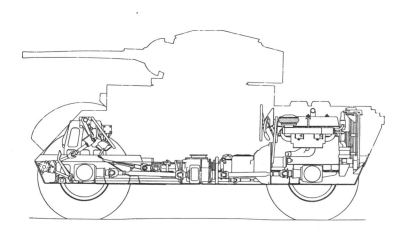

Armored Car, Daimler Mark I   (Great Britain)

Weight	8.4 short tons, 7.5 long tons (7.6 tons)
Length	13 ft. 5 in. (4.09 m)
Width	8 ft. (2.44 m)
Height	7 ft. 4 in. (2.23 m)
Engine	Daimler, 6-cylinder, watercooled, 100 h.p., 3,600 r.p.m.
Speed	50 m.p.h. (80 km.p.h.)
Tank capacity . .	43.2 U.S. gal., 36 Imp. gal. (163 l)
Armament . . .	1 40-mm (2 pdr) Ordnance QF Mk. II or Mk. IXA, 2 mg, smoke discharger
Ammunition . .	52 2-pdr rds, 3,200 mg rds, 9 smoke candles
Range	205 miles (330 km)
Armor	14 mm, turret 16 mm
Number in series .	2,694 of both Mark I and Mark II
Year	1941

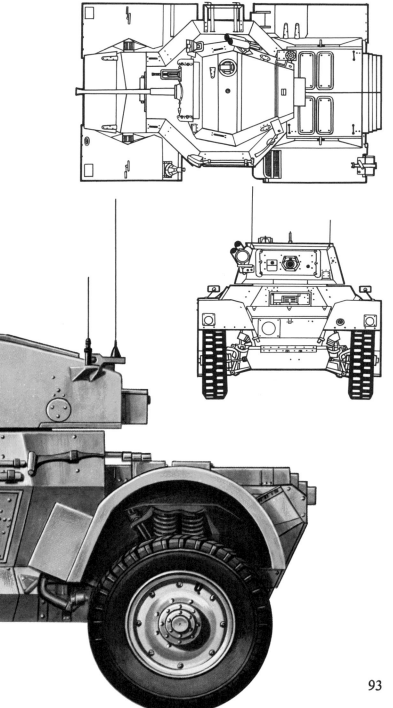

The American M3A1 armored personnel carrier, one of the most reliable half-track vehicles used by the Allies.

An invention by the French engineer Adolphe Kégresse made the construction of half-track vehicles a practical proposition. By fitting the track with rubber studs he obtained a track-laying system that could be employed on ordinary roads. It was first utilized on a Peugeot and subsequently on various Citroëns. The Germans adopted it on their Sd machines and the American half-track M3 became world-famous. These armored personnel carriers (APC) appeared in every theatre of World War II. Over 22,000 were built in various factories; some were in service in Britain until 1967 while others are still employed by the Israeli forces.

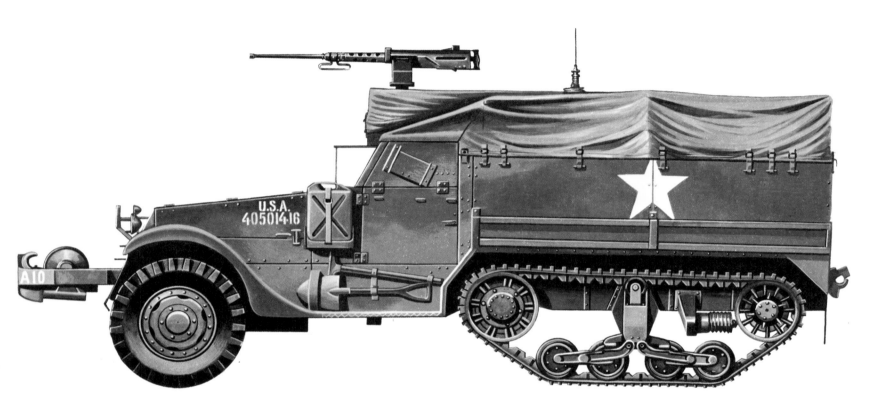

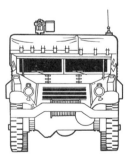

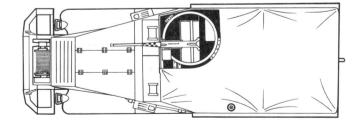

Armored Personnel Carrier (APC),   (U.S.A.) M3 Half-Track

Weight	8.5 short tons, 7.5 long tons (7.7 tons)
Length	20 ft. 2 ⅝ in. (6.16 m)
Width	7 ft. 3 ½ in. (2.22 m)
Height	7 ft. 5 in. (2.26 m)
Engine	White 160 AX, 6-cylinder, watercooled, 147 h.p., 3,000 r.p.m.
Speed	45–55 m.p.h. (72–88 km.p.h.)
Tank capacity . .	60 U.S. gal., 50 Imp. gal. (227.4 l)
Range	180–215 miles (290–346 km)
Armament . . .	1 Browning M1919 mg, 1 carbine
Ammunition . .	4,000 mg rds (M3A1 7,750 additional rds for .30-calibre mg)
Armor	6.3–12.7 mm
Crew	13
Number in series .	22,837 of all types
Year	1941–44

Until well into 1943 the Soviet T34 was "the best tank in the world"—that, at least, was the opinion expressed by General Guderian—and the Russians continued to build T34s until 1964. Innumerable tales are told about them. One is that some ran off the assembly lines right up to the front driven by women, who made up a large part of the labor force in the Russian armament factories. Even towards the end of the war, when the T34 had lost its superiority in the field to more up-to-date German vehicles, the numbers thrown into battle often made the difference between defeat and victory. Whereas in 1940 only 115 T34s were produced, between 1943 and 1945 10,000 rolled off the assembly lines every year. The driving system of the T34 was derived from Christie's and the relatively light machine—it weighed less than 27 tons—could travel without the track where the terrain was firm enough to bear its weight. Western observers criticized the T34 because crew accommodation was wretched and radio was installed in only a very few command vehicles. Nonetheless, the truth is that this was one of the first really successful tanks in the history of war.

Tank, T34/76   (Soviet Union)

Weight	29.7 short tons, 26.6 long tons (27 tons)
Length	21 ft. 7 in. (6.58 m)
Width.	9 ft. 10 in. (3 m)
Height	8 ft. (2.44 m)
Engine	V2, 12-cylinder Diesel, watercooled, 500 h.p., 1,800 r.p.m.
Speed.	32 m.p.h. (51 km.p.h.)
Tank capacity. .	162 U.S. gal., 135 Imp. gal. (614 l) in 8 tanks, additional fuel in extra, removable tanks
Armament . . .	1 76.2-mm cannon, 2 mg
Ammunition . .	77 cannon rds, 2,000–3,000 mg rds
Armor	45 mm, turret 65 mm
Crew	4
Number in series .	About 40,000 of all models
Year	From June 1940

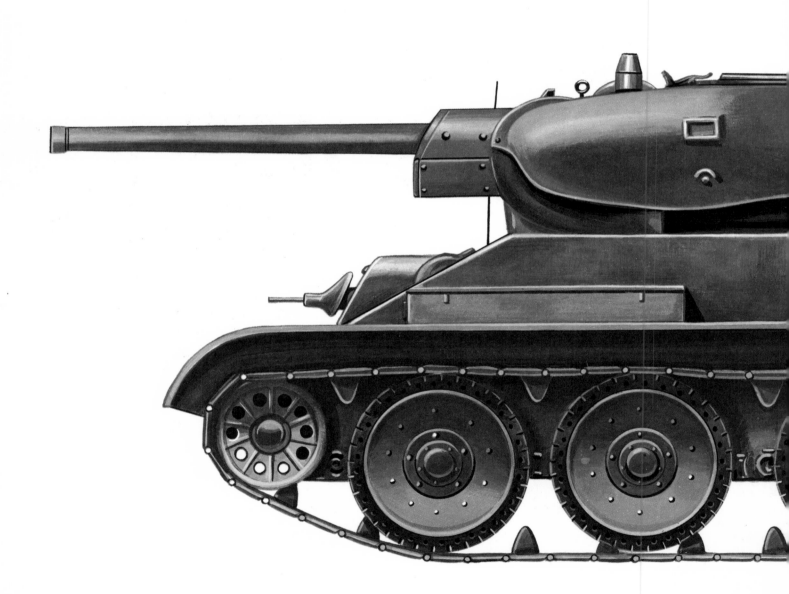

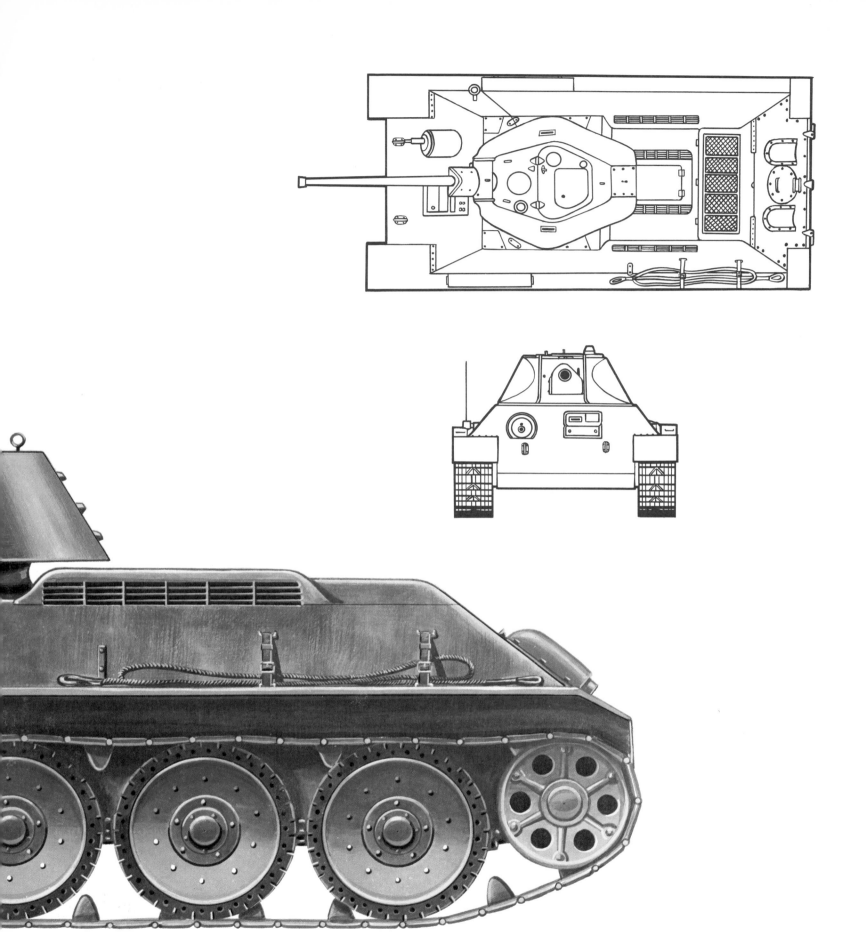

The German P I, P II and P III were at a disadvantage during the first year of the war and could do little against the heavier British, French and Russian tanks. For that reason in May 1941 Hitler demanded a sufficiently heavy tank for his army. The new vehicle should be able to find its target at a range of 1,600 yards and penetrate 4-inch armor plating. Prototypes were submitted by Henschel and Porsche. The former got the order and started production of the P VI, which was first called "Tiger Model E" and later simply "Tiger I". Henschel had had some experience of tank production in the thirties and as a result the Tiger incorporated some features of earlier experimental models, such as the "breakthrough vehicle" of which two specimens were built in 1937. It was equipped with the famous 88-mm cannon and was the first mass-produced tank to have overlapping wheels. By November 1942 only 13 had been built, but after that production reached 25 or more a month. Total output of Tiger Is was 1,350. The Tiger I first saw action before Leningrad in September 1942 and was subsequently used in North Africa, in Italy and, towards the end of the war, on all the fronts round about Germany. For some time it was considered even by experts as the best tank in the field.

PzKpfw VI Ausführung E, Tiger I (Sd. Kfz. 181)   (Germany)

Weight	62.7 short tons, 56 long tons (57 tons)
Length	27 ft. 9 in. (8.46 m)
Width	12 ft. 3 in. (3.73 m)
Height	9 ft. 6 in. (2.9 m)
Engine	Maybach HL 210 P 45, 12-cylinder, watercooled, 650 h.p., 2,500–3,000 r.p.m.
Speed	12–23 m.p.h. (19–37 km.p.h.)
Tank capacity . .	150 U.S. gal., 125 Imp. gal. (567 l)
Range	42–73 miles (67–117 km)
Armament . . .	1 88-mm KwK 36, 2 mg, 6 smoke dischargers
Ammunition . .	92 88-mm rds, 5,700 mg rds, 39 smoke candles
Armor	100 mm, turret 110 mm
Crew	5
Number in series .	1,350 of all types
Year	1942–45

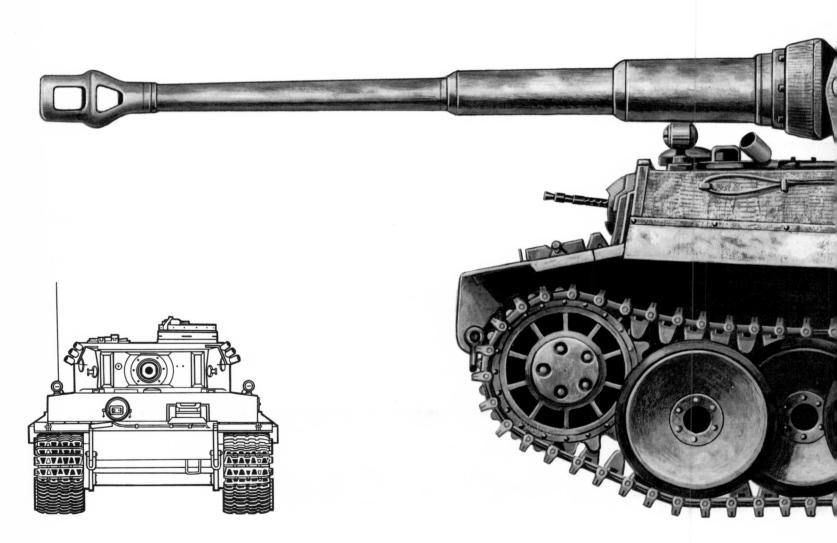

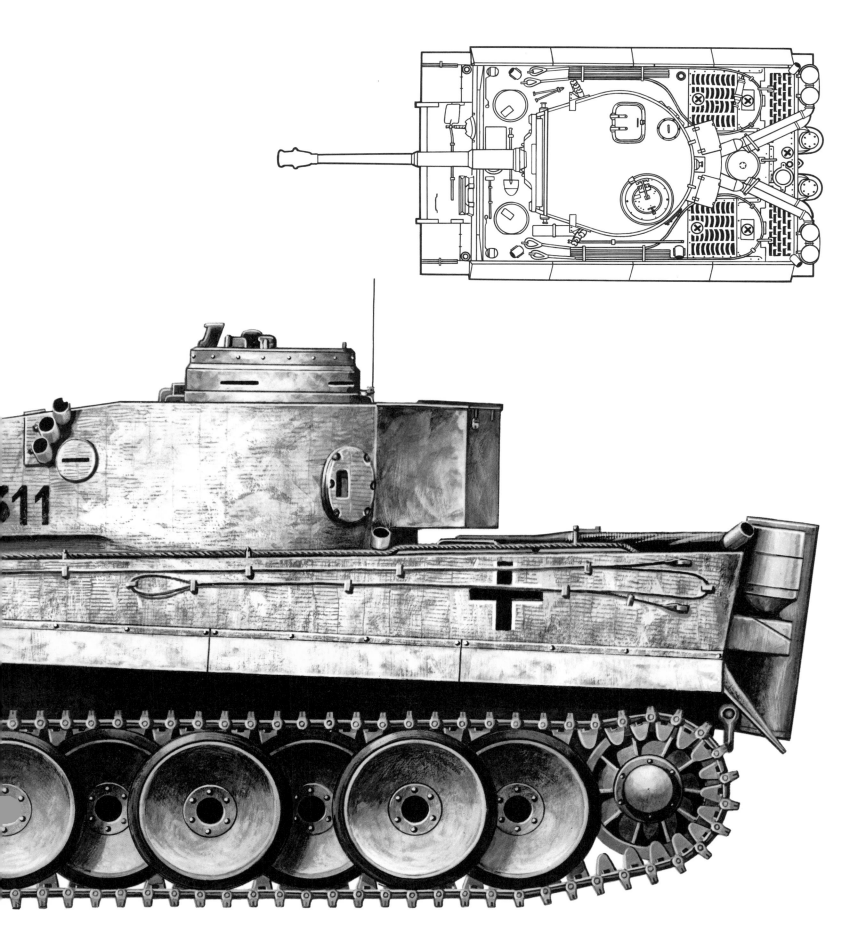

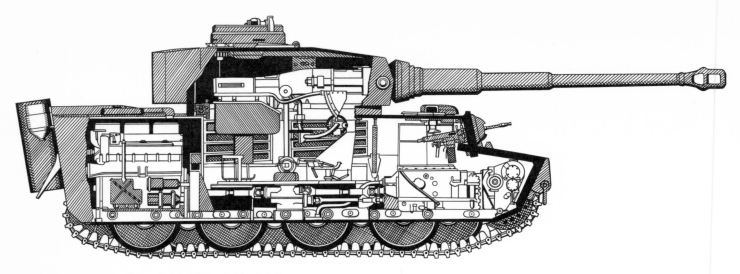

Cross-section of the P VI, Tiger I Model E.

Its 88-mm cannon gave the German Tiger I greater fighting power than most of its opponents could boast of. Its armor plating was also in advance of the times.

The Tiger I, which appeared in 1942, was built to combat the Russian T34s.

in France. The principles formulated by Guderian, who found in de Gaulle a French strategist who shared his views, were clearly demonstrated as correct. The German High Command had learnt to employ tanks in close formation and give them a free rein.

The tanks constructed between 1939 and 1940 were well adapted for a lightning war. As the war progressed it had become more and more painfully evident that light tanks were particularly susceptible to antitank guns and they were soon replaced on the battlefield by heavier vehicles. Tanks became quite rapidly diversified and evolved towards specific shapes and functions:
— the combat tank, heavily armored, armed with a high velocity cannon;
— the large-caliber, high velocity assault gun, heavily armored in front; this was in fact the artillery that accompanied tank units;
— the tank destroyer, lightly armored, armed with a very powerful antitank gun capable of long-range firing.

By the end of the hostilities tanks had become powerful weapons; their engines had greater horsepower, transmission and tracks had been improved, radio had entered into common use and the vehicles were easier to drive.

The combat tank began the war in triumph but in spite of the progressive improvements made on it the development of antitank weapons and mines made it lose its independence in the face of other arms, particularly those of the infantry. At the end of the war the problem arose as to whether tank protection should be reinforced or whether the fight against mobility and fire power should be abandoned altogether.

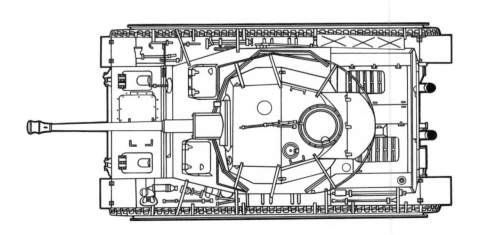

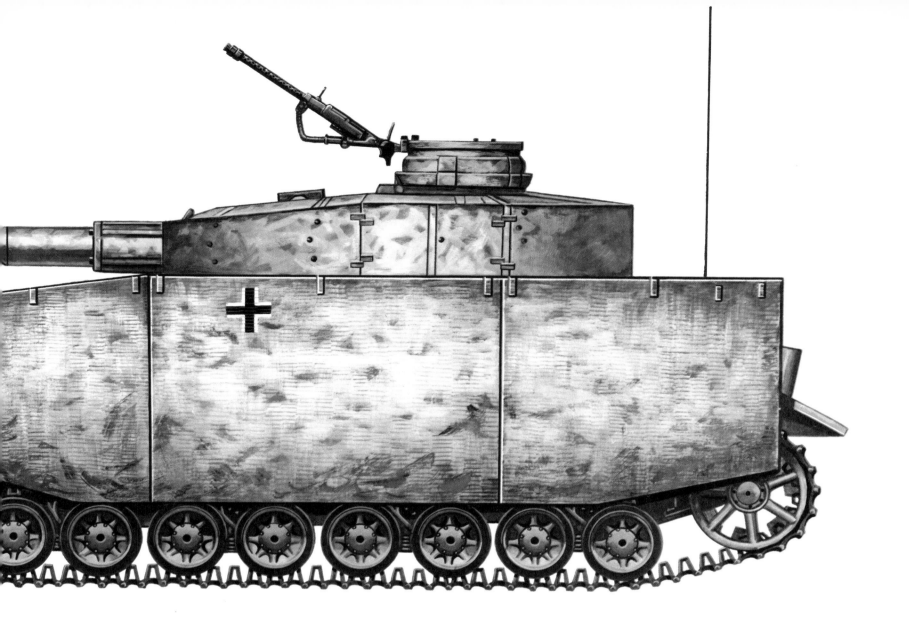

The P IV, which belonged to the 20-ton class and was equipped with a 75-mm cannon, completed the German tank range. First designed as an infantry support vehicle, it was mass-produced in 1937 as the major weapon of the German tank corps. And when the P III was dropped in 1943, production of the P IV continued. All in all, some 850 tanks of this type were built and they were employed right up to the end of the war. Through the years various alterations were introduced and the same chassis was used for command tanks, bridge-laying tanks and even for simple supply vehicles. Some tanks were specially equipped for fording watercourses up to 13 feet deep.

PzKpfw IV, Ausführung J (Sd. Kfz. 161)   (Germany)

Weight	27.5 short tons, 24.6 long tons (25 tons)
Length	23 ft. 4 ½ in. (7.02 m)
Width	10 ft. 5 in. (3.18 m)
Height	8 ft. 10 in. (2.68 m)
Engine	Maybach HL 120 TRM, 12-cylinder, watercooled, 300 h.p., 3,000 r.p.m.
Speed	15–24 m.p.h. (24–38 km.p.h.)
Tank capacity . .	179 U.S. gal., 149 Imp. gal. (680 l)
Range	131–200 miles (210–320 km)
Armament . . .	1 75-mm KwK 40 1/48, 2 mg
Ammunition . .	87 75-mm rds, 3,150 mg rds
Armor	80 mm, turret 30 mm
Crew	5
Number in series .	About 6,000 of H and J models
Year	1937–45

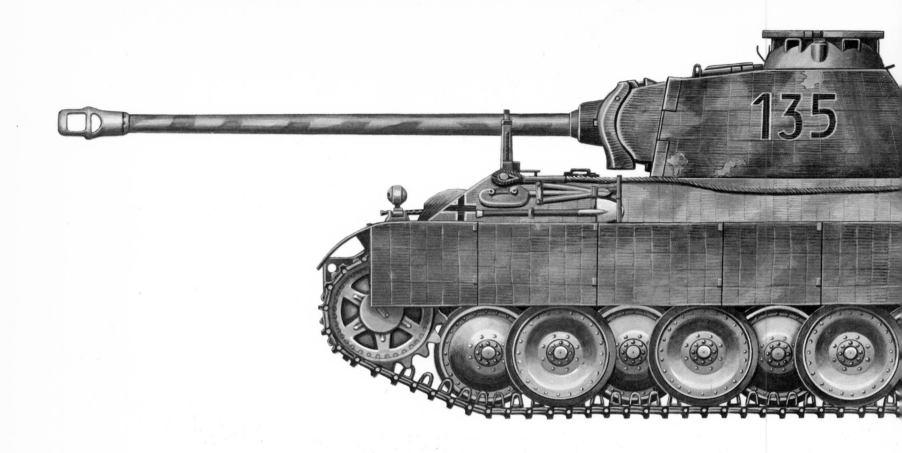

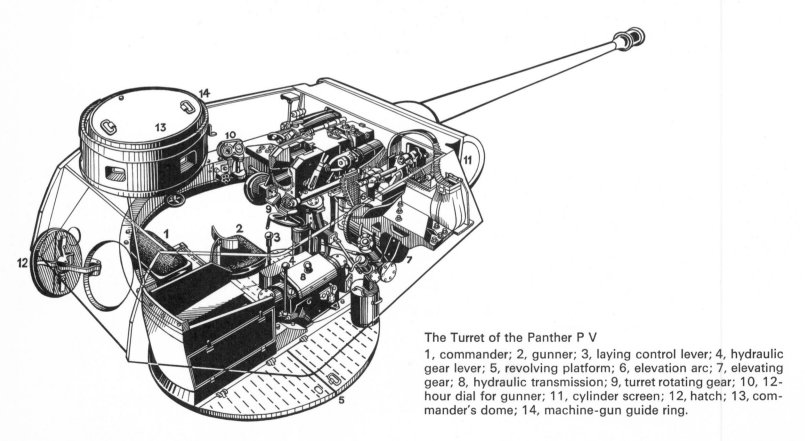

The Turret of the Panther P V

1, commander; 2, gunner; 3, laying control lever; 4, hydraulic gear lever; 5, revolving platform; 6, elevation arc; 7, elevating gear; 8, hydraulic transmission; 9, turret rotating gear; 10, 12-hour dial for gunner; 11, cylinder screen; 12, hatch; 13, commander's dome; 14, machine-gun guide ring.

The P V, known as the "Panther", was the first German answer to the Russian T34, which the German armored troops first encountered on July 2, 1941. They got such a drubbing that a few months later a team of German experts was sent to the Eastern front and made a thorough study of the T34. Prototypes were submitted by two German tank manufacturers in 1942. The army preferred the MAN model but Hitler decided in favour of the Daimler-Benz. The first consignment reached the troops in mid-1943. The "Panther" was one of the most successful German tanks and one of the best of all those that appeared during World War II. The different specialized versions (command, tank-recovery, mine-sweeping, etc.) added up to a total of 5,805 in all.

PzKpfw V Panther Ausführung G (Germany) (Sd. Kfz. 171)

Weight	49.3 short tons, 40.6 long tons (44.8 tons)
Length	29 ft. 0 ¾ in. (8.86 m)
Width.	10 ft. 8 ¾ in. (3.27 m)
Height	9 ft. 10 in. (2.99 m)
Engine	Maybach HL 230 P 30, 12-cylinder, watercooled, 700 h.p., 3,000 r.p.m.
Speed.	15–24 m.p.h. (25–46 km.p.h.)
Tank capacity. .	193 U.S. gal., 160 Imp. gal. (730 l)
Range.	62 miles, cross-country (100 km) 124 miles, road (200 km)
Armament . . .	1 75-mm cannon KwK 42, 2 mg
Ammunition . .	82 75-mm rds, 4,200 mg rds
Armor	80 mm, turret 100 mm
Crew	5
Number in series .	3,740
Year	1943–45

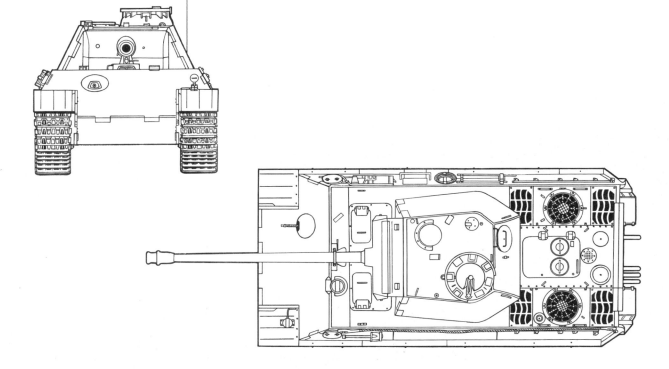

The British "Valentine" infantry tank weighed only 16 tons, so it was not much more than an escort vehicle. But during the last phase of the North African campaign it frequently did duty as an assault tank with very good results. It got its name from the fact that the British firm of Vickers Armstrong submitted the plans for their tank on St Valentine's Day, 1938, though not officially requested to do so by the War Office. Valentines started to come off the assembly line in 1940; by 1944 8,275 had been delivered to the armed forces, of which one-fifth assembled in Canada. A large number were supplied to the Red Army.

Infantry Tank, Mark III,   (Great Britain)
Valentine II

Weight	17.9 short tons, 16 long tons (16.3 tons)
Length	17 ft. 9 in. (5.4 m)
Width	8 ft. 7 ½ in. (2.63 m)
Height	7 ft. 5 ½ in. (2.27 m)
Engine	A.E.C. Type A.190 Diesel, 6-cylinder 131 h.p., 1,800 r.p.m.
Speed	15 m.p.h. (24 km.p.h.)
Tank capacity . .	43.2 U.S. gal., 36 Imp. gal. (163.6 l)
Range	90 miles (145 km)
Armament . . .	1 2-pdr Ordnance QF Mk. IX or X, 1 mg, 1 smoke discharger (1 additional mg)
Ammunition . .	60 2-pdr rds, 3,150 mg rds, 18 smoke candles (600 additional mg rds)
Armor	65 mm
Crew	3
Number in series .	8,275 of all types
Year	1940–43

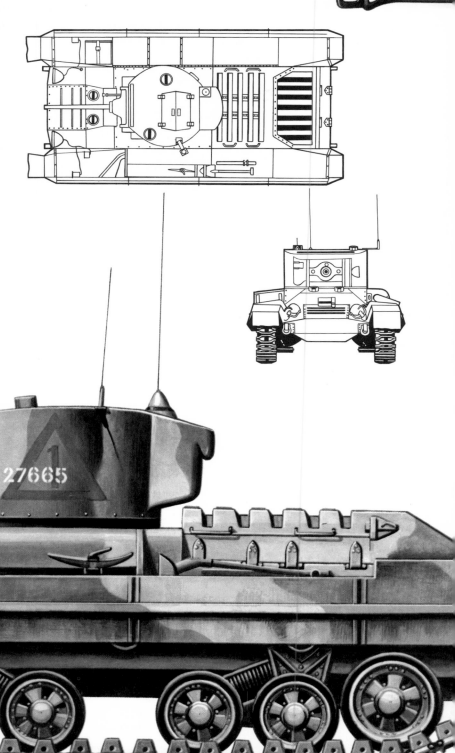

T27665

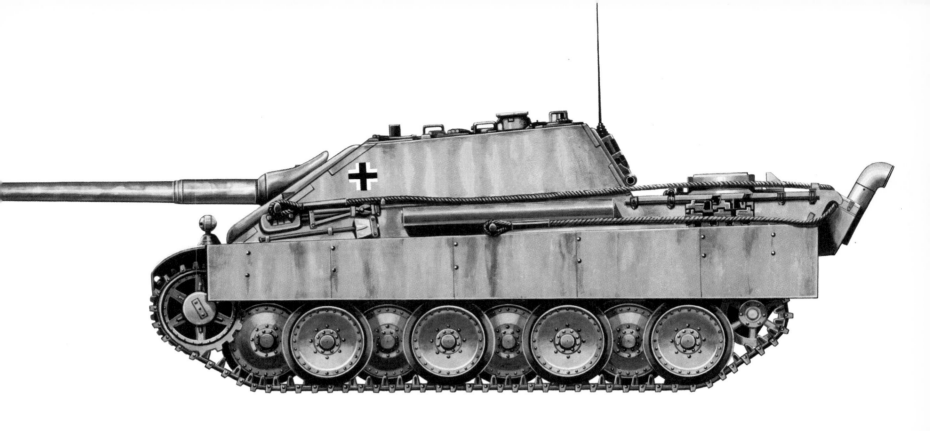

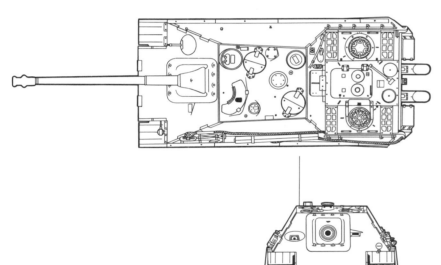

The "Jagdpanther" (Fighter Panther) was a Panther without a turret—a dangerous ambush machine that carried an 88-mm gun instead of the standard model's 77-mm. A total of 230 were built between 1943 and 1944. Though basically not very mobile, this powerful tank was such a success that there was an idea of mounting a 128-mm cannon on it, an improvement that never got beyond the planning stage.

Jagdpanzer (Sd. Kfz. 173)   (Germany)

Weight	50.05 short tons, 44.8 long tons (45.5 tons)
Length	33 ft. 1 in. (10.10 m)
Width	10 ft. 9 in. (3.27 m)
Height	8 ft. 11 in. (2.72 m)
Engine	Maybach HL 230 P 30, 12-cylinder, watercooled, 700 h.p., 3,000 r.p.m.
Speed	15–28 m.p.h. (24–46 km.p.h.)
Tank capacity . .	190.2 U.S. gal., 158.4 Imp. gal. (720 l)
Range	50–100 miles (80–160 km)
Armament . . .	1 88 Pak 43/3, L/71, 1 mg
Ammunition . .	60 88-mm rds, 6,000 mg rds
Armor	80 mm
Crew	5
Number built . .	384
Year	1943–45

The German P IV was employed from 1939 to 1945. Ten
different versions were built.

The British Mark VIII "Cromwell IV" passed all its tests with
flying colours before being delivered to the troops.

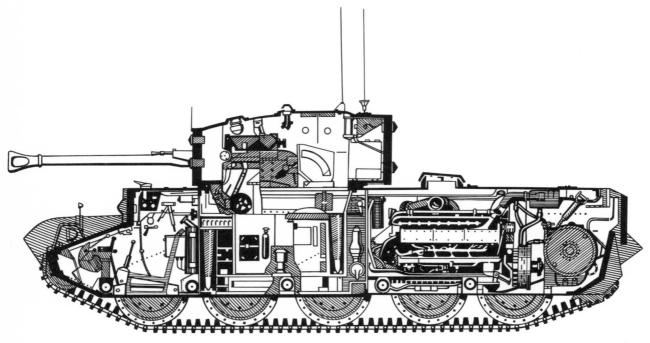

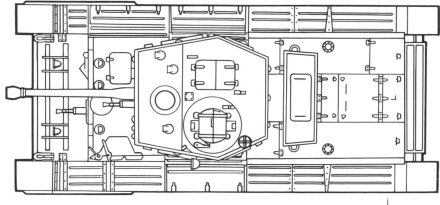

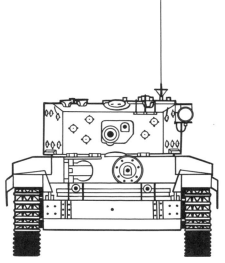

A27(M), Cruiser Mark VIII, Cromwell IV (Great Britain)

Weight	30.8 short tons, 27.5 long tons (28 tons)
Length	20 ft. 10 in. (6.35 m)
Width	9 ft. 6 ½ in. (2.9 m)
Height	8 ft. 3 in. (2.51 m)
Engine	Rolls-Royce Meteor, 12-cylinder, water-cooled, 570–600 h.p., 2,500 r.p.m.
Speed	38 m.p.h. (61 km.p.h.)
Tank capacity . .	139.2 U.S. gal., 116 Imp. gal. (527 l) in 2 tanks (additional tank 30 gal.)
Range	81–174 miles (130–280 km)
Armament . . .	1 75-mm QF Mk.V or Mk.VA, 2 mg, 1 smoke discharger
Ammunition . .	64–75 75-mm rds, 4,950 mg rds, 30 smoke candles
Armor	76 mm
Crew	5
Number in series .	Produced in large numbers
Year	1943–45

One of the most successful British tanks was the "Cromwell", a medium tank derived from the "Crusader" and the final member of the series of British battle tanks designed to achieve a tactical breakthrough. Cromwells armed with a 95-mm howitzer served as infantry support vehicles, but the latest models had a 75-mm cannon. They had a crew of five and their strong point was their great mobility, thanks to which they were often victorious over heavier tanks. Cromwells were first employed at the Normandy landings and the last time they saw action was in the Korean War.

This 8-wheeled heavy reconnaissance car "Puma" carried a 50-mm cannon and its 220-h.p. engine gave it a top speed of some 60 m.p.h. A total of 2,300 of these vehicles was built by a number of firms to various specifications. The armored reconnaissance car was one of the most modern vehicles built during World War II: its range of action made it extremely useful for tank troop commanders.

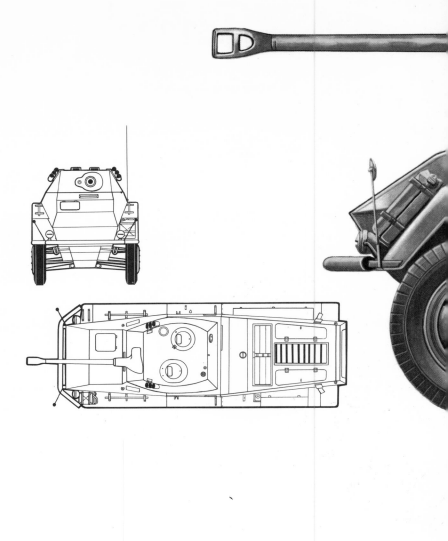

Heavy Armored Car, Puma (Germany) (Sd. Kfz. 234/2)

Weight	12.1 short tons, 10.8 long tons (11 tons)
Length	22 ft. 3 ½ in. (6.8 m) (including gun)
Width	7 ft. 8 in. (2.38 m)
Height	7 ft. 10 in. (2.33 m)
Engine	Tatra "III", 12-cylinder, Diesel, 220 h.p.
Speed	56 m.p.h. (90 km.p.h.)
Tank capacity . .	95.13 U.S. gal., 79.1 Imp. gal. (360 l)
Range	621 miles (1,000 km)
Armament . . .	1 50-mm KwK 39/1 L60, 1 mg
Ammunition . .	55 50-mm rds, 2,850 mg rds
Armor	30 mm
Crew	4
Number in series .	2,300 of the Sd. Kfz. 234 series
Year	1944

The "Elephant" was very effective, though only used in small numbers by the German forces. It derived from the Tiger and was first called "Ferdinand" after Ferdinand Porsche who was responsible for the design. As a fighter tank in the narrowest sense of the term, its task was to lie in wait well camouflaged until it could let fly with its heavy, flat-trajectory cannon. But it was not sufficiently mobile —on this point it well deserved its name—and was soon left behind by the Jagdpanther.

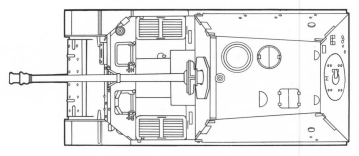

Jagdpanzer Tiger (P) Elephant (Germany) (Sd. Kfz. 184)

Weight	74.8 short tons, 66.9 long tons (68 tons)
Length	22 ft. 3 ½ in. (6.8 m) excluding gun
Width	11 ft. 3 in. (3.43 m)
Height	10 ft. 6 in. (3.2 m)
Engine	2 Maybach, HL 120 TRM, 12-cylinder, watercooled and each 320 h.p., 3,000 r.p.m.
Speed	22 m.p.h. (35 km.p.h.)
Tank capacity . .	About 290.6 U.S. gal., 241.9 Imp. gal. (1,100 l)
Range	49 miles (80 km)
Armament . . .	1 88-mm Pak 43/2 L/71, 1 mg
Armor	200 mm
Crew	6
Number in series .	90
Year	1943

112

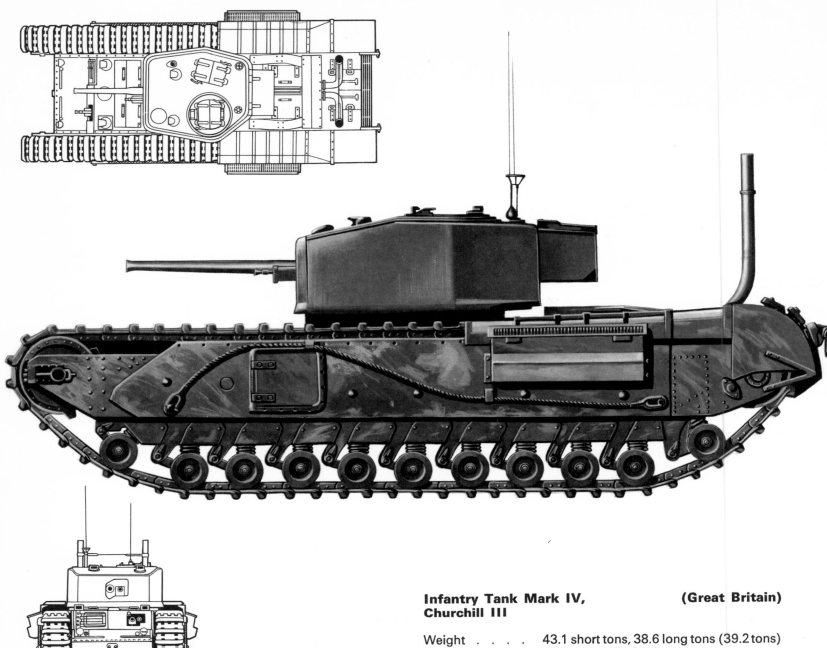

The "Churchill", an improvement on the British Mark IV infantry tank—which never reached the production stage— weighed over 39 tons in battle trim and was designed to break through the static front that was expected to become established along the French Maginot and the German Siegfried Lines. It was developed in an amazingly short time. On August 19, 1942, a Canadian regiment supported by 28 Churchills attempted a landing at Dieppe. Equipped for negotiating rather deep coastal waters, only six managed to penetrate the shore defenses: they were repulsed. In spite of this unfortunate début the Churchill succeeded in asserting itself. Of this tank 5,640 were built, putting it second only to the Valentine in numbers.

Infantry Tank Mark IV, Churchill III   (Great Britain)

Weight	43.1 short tons, 38.6 long tons (39.2 tons)
Length	24 ft. 5 in. (7.43 m)
Width	10 ft. 8 in. (3.25 m)
Height	8 ft. 2 in. (2.49 m)
Engine	Bedford Twin-Six, 12-cylinder, 350 h.p., 2,200 r.p.m.
Speed	15 m.p.h. (25 km.p.h.)
Tank capacity	219 U.S. gal., 182.5 Imp. gal. (830 l) in 6 tanks
Range	120 miles (193 km)
Armament	1 6-pdr (57-mm) Ordnance QF, 2 mg, 1 smoke discharger
Ammunition	84 6-pdr rds, 9,450 mg rds, 30 smoke candles
Armor	88 mm
Crew	5
Number in series	5,640 of all models
Year	1940–41 (later Marks were in production until 1945)

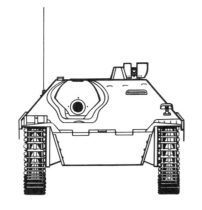

In 1943 the German High Command turned its attention to an extremely mobile light pursuit tank. The occupation of Czechoslovakia had given Germany control over the Skoda works, whose tanks were renowned for their very modern chassis. The "Hetzer" (Chaser) was remarkable for its flat silhouette; its outstanding features were fire power and mobility. After the second world war Hetzers were put into service by the Swiss army.

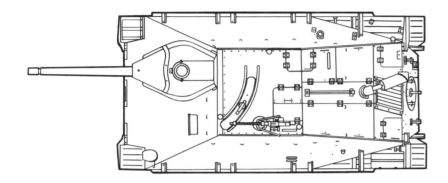

Jagdpanzer 38(t) Hetzer (Germany)

Weight	17.6 short tons, 15.72 long tons (16 tons)
Length	20 ft. 7 in. (6.27 m) (including gun)
Width	8 ft. 8 ½ in. (2.65 m)
Height	6 ft. 11 ½ in. (2.11 m)
Engine	Praga, 6-cylinder, watercooled, 150 h.p., 2,600 r.p.m.
Speed	26 m.p.h. (42 km.p.h.)
Tank capacity . .	85 U.S. gal., 70.8 Imp. gal. (322 l)
Range	80–130 miles (129–209 km)
Armament . . .	1 75 Pak 39 L/48, 1 mg
Ammunition . .	41 75-mm rds, 600 mg rds
Armor	60 mm
Crew	4
Number in series .	1,577
Year	1944–45

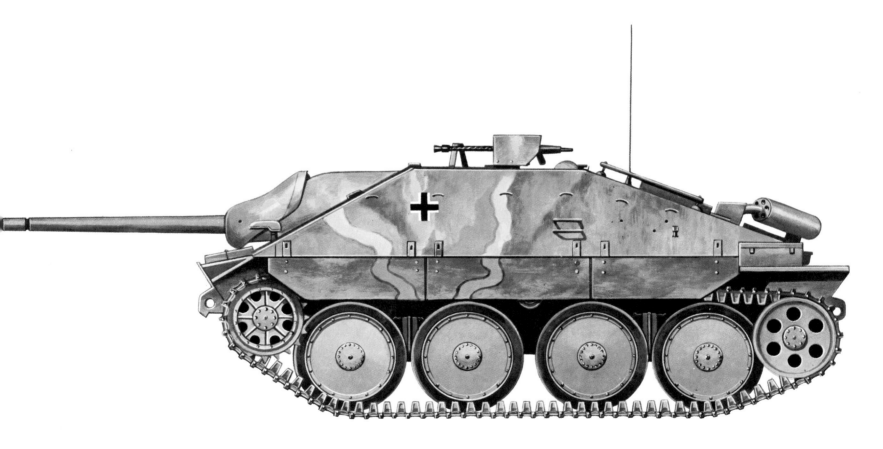

Street fighting in Budapest during the Hungarian uprising in
1956. Two Russian JSU152s and one T34/85.

116

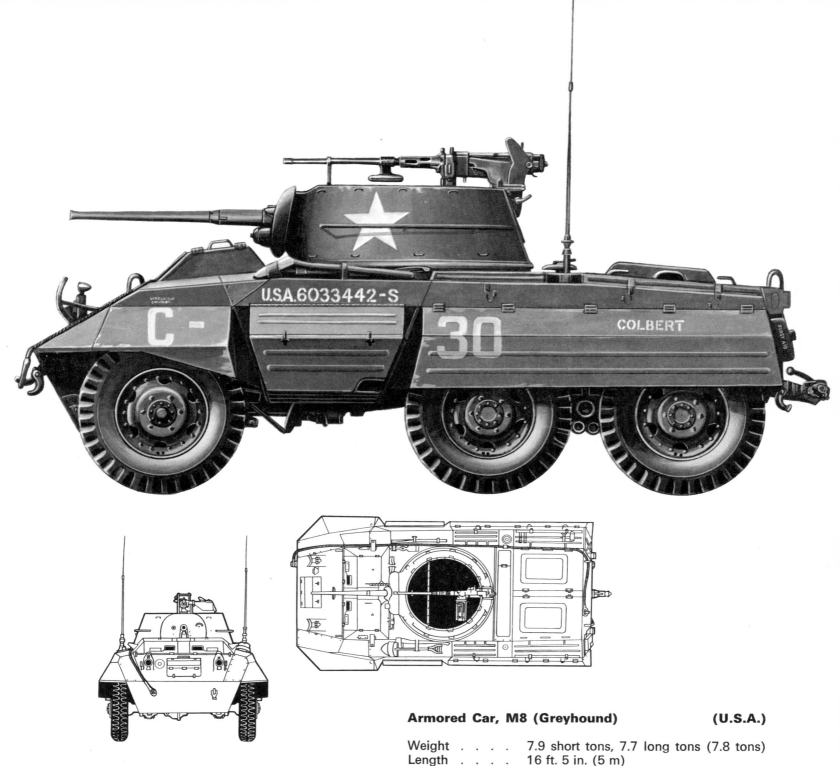

The American M8 armored car was the Allied answer to the German Puma. Experts said it could neither win a race nor decide a battle. However, the M8 proved extremely successful as tank-age cavalry and as a pursuit vehicle. In 1943 it was adopted by the British, who called it the Greyhound and used it in Africa and Europe. After the war the M8 served the tank corps of various NATO countries for many years. Today, with a few technical innovations and a different superstructure, the 8-ton armored car is still used for "police work" in the United States.

Armored Car, M8 (Greyhound)   **(U.S.A.)**

Weight	7.9 short tons, 7.7 long tons (7.8 tons)
Length	16 ft. 5 in. (5 m)
Width	8 ft. 4 in. (2.54 m)
Height	7 ft. 4 ½ in. (2.25 m)
Engine	Hercules JXD, 6-cylinder, 110 h.p., 3,000 r.p.m.
Speed	55 m.p.h. (88 km.p.h.)
Tank capacity . .	69 U.S. gal., 57 Imp. gal. (261 l)
Range	350 miles (563 km)
Armament . . .	1 37-mm M6 cannon, 2 mg
Ammunition . .	16–80 cannon rds, 1,900 mg rds
Armor	25 mm
Crew	4
Number in series .	Produced in large numbers
Year	1943–45

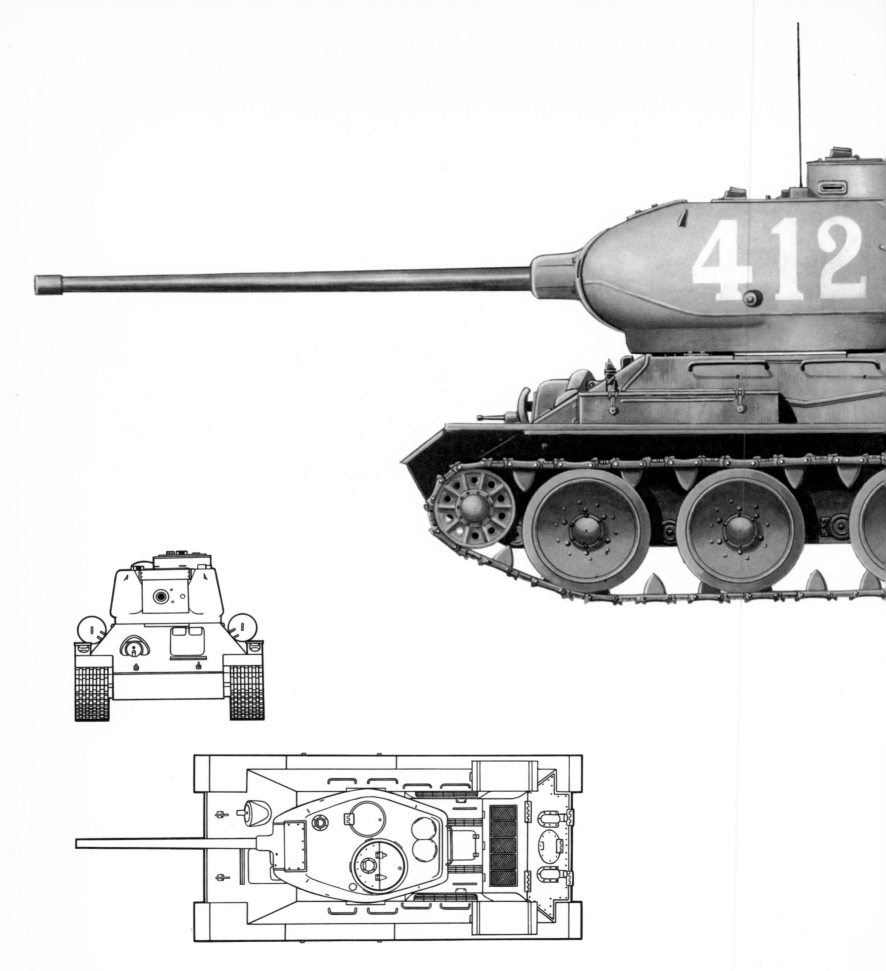

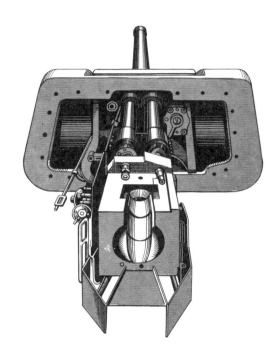

The 85-mm cannon L53 of the T34/85.

The Russian T34/85 was the last member of the T34 series. It carried an 85-mm cannon, which made it a match for any German tank. It first appeared on the front in 1943 in ones and twos and was used as an infantry support vehicle. A year later production had been boosted enormously. The T34/85 weighed about 31 tons but its range of action was less than 200 miles. An interesting feature was the fuel tanks, which were located outside the vehicle behind the turret.

Tank, T34/85 (U.S.S.R.)

Weight	34.4 short tons, 30.8 long tons (31.3 tons)
Length	20 ft. 2 in. (6.15 m) (excluding gun)
Width	9 ft. 9 in. (2.97 m)
Engine	V.2 Diesel, 12-cylinder (V-12), 500 h.p., 1,800 r.p.m.
Speed	32 m.p.h. (51 km.p.h.)
Tank capacity . .	147 U.S. gal., 122.5 Imp. gal. (557 l) in 8 tanks, plus 2 external tanks
Range	155–250 miles (249–402 km)
Armament . . .	1 85-mm gun SiS 53, 2 mg
Ammunition . .	56 85-mm rds, 1,890 mg rds
Armor	75 mm, turret 95 mm
Crew	5
Number in series .	Produced in large numbers
Year	1943–45

During the Battle of Berlin in 1945 the Russians threw their
SU100 self-propelled gun into the fray.

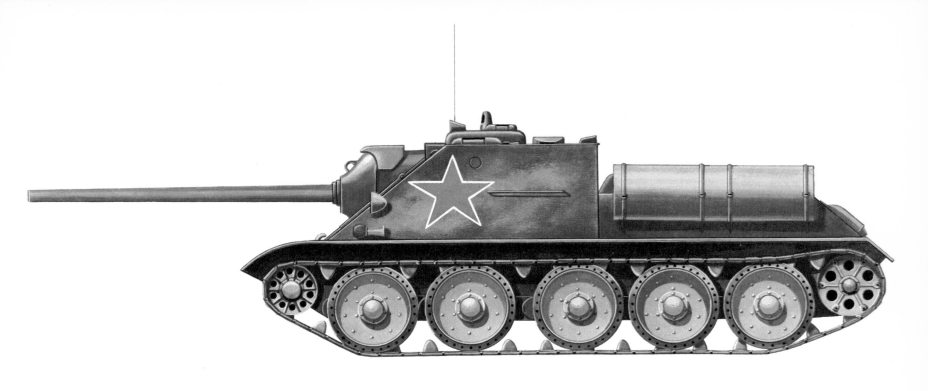

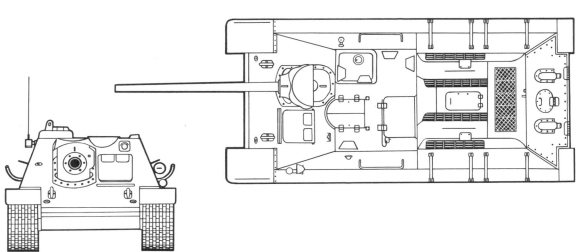

Assault Gun, SU85   **(U.S.S.R.)**

Weight	32.4 short tons, 28.9 long tons (29.5 tons)
Length	26 ft. 8 in. (8.13 m)
Width	9 ft. 10 ½ in. (3 m)
Height	7 ft. 9 in. (2.36 m)
Engine	V.2 Diesel, 12-cylinder (V-12), water-cooled, 500 h.p., 1,800 r.p.m.
Speed	34 m.p.h. (55 km.p.h.)
Tank capacity . .	162 U.S. gal., 135 Imp. gal. (613.2 l) in 8 tanks
Range	186 miles (299 km)
Armament . . .	1 85-mm DS-S 85
Ammunition . .	48 85-mm rds
Armor	20–45 mm
Crew	5
Number in series .	Produced in large numbers
Year	1943

When the Russians saw how efficient the German pursuit tanks were they decided to build one of their own. For this purpose they mounted their newly developed 85-mm cannon on the chassis of the trusty T34. The result was the SU85 "Samokhodnaya Ustanovka" (Self-propelled Gun), which appeared in 1944. A year later, in 1945—the last year of the war—it was followed by a specially designed vehicle armed with a 100-mm cannon. Immediately after the war the SU85 was handed over to the Soviet satellite countries.

The American M4 "Sherman" tank is still a bone of contention among military experts. The outcome of the war did not afford adequate proof as to whether it was better than the German tanks that went into battle just before hostilities came to an end. One fact is certain: thanks to its extraordinarily mobile turret, the Sherman could hit much faster. Another fact is that the American tank units could rely on a service organization that was unique at the time. The overwhelming victory of the Allies on the Western front would not have been possible without the Sherman, which was employed by a dozen different armies. From 1942 to 1945 48,071 M4s were built, including over 11,000 of the famous A3 model. After the war the Sherman became the standard tank of the NATO forces. The American army used it—in Korea it came to grips with the Russian T34/85—until 1955, when it was superseded by the Patton. Shermans chalked up their most recent victories in June 1967, when the Israelis employed them successfully against Russian tanks crewed by the Egyptians during the Six Day War.

Medium Tank, M4A3 (76 mm)   **(U.S.A.)**
MVSS Sherman

Weight	37.1 short tons, 33.2 long tons (33.8 tons)
Length	19 ft. 3 in. (5.86 m)
Width	9 ft. 8 in. (2.94 m)
Height	9 ft. 9 in. (2.96 m)
Engine	Ford GAA-III, 8-cylinder, watercooled, 450 h.p., 2,600 r.p.m.
Speed	30 m.p.h. (48 km.p.h.)
Tank capacity . .	168 U.S. gal., 140 Imp. gal. (636 l)
Range	120 miles (193 km)
Armament . . .	1 76 M1A1C or M1A2 gun, 3 mg, 12-in. mortar
Ammunition . .	71 76-mm rds, 6,850 mg rds, 12 mortar rds
Armor	62 mm
Crew	5
Number in series .	About 49,000 of all types
Year	1942–45

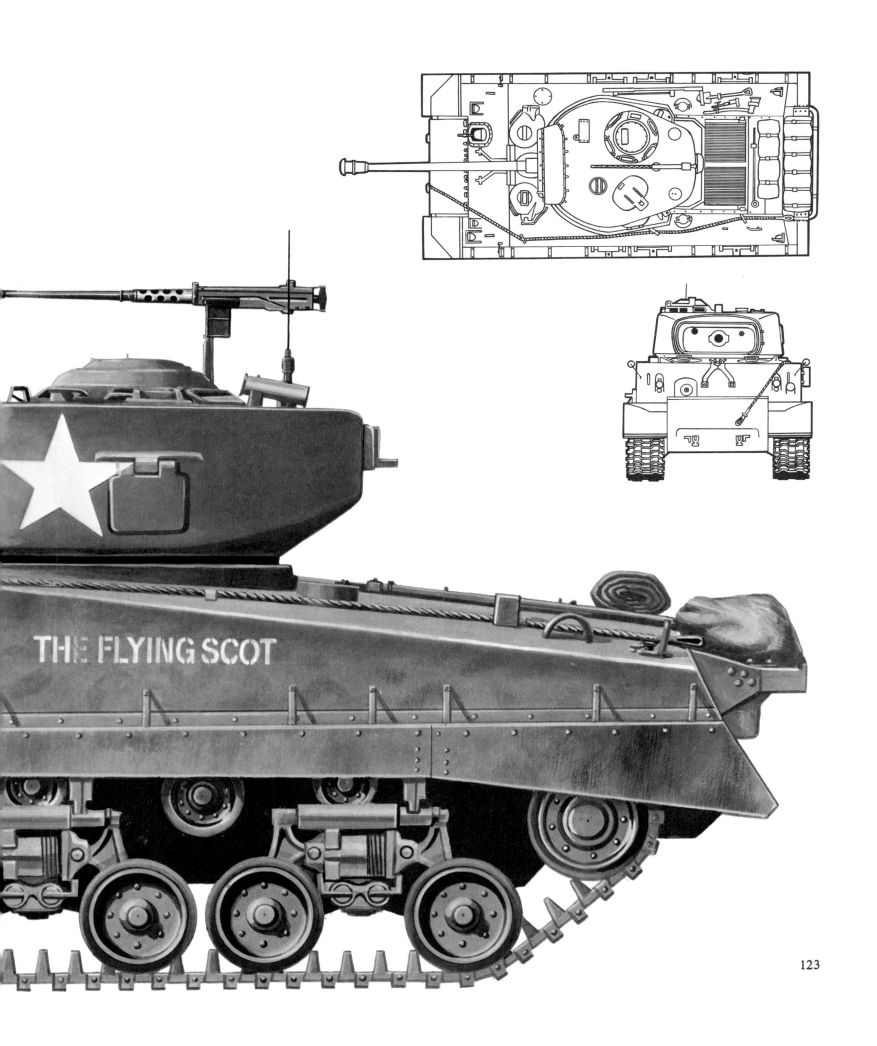

THE FLYING SCOT

American Sherman VC "Firefly" with Polish volunteers in
the Dutch town of Moerdijk in November 1944.

The German 70-ton Tiger II was not very mobile but its magnificent cannon often made it victorious in tank duels.

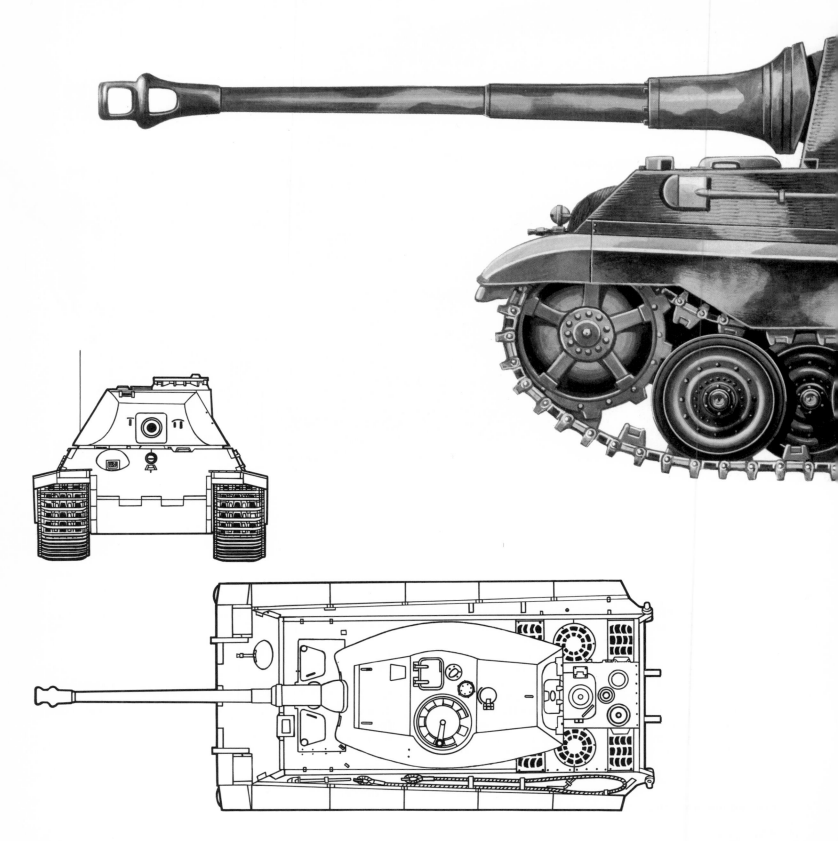

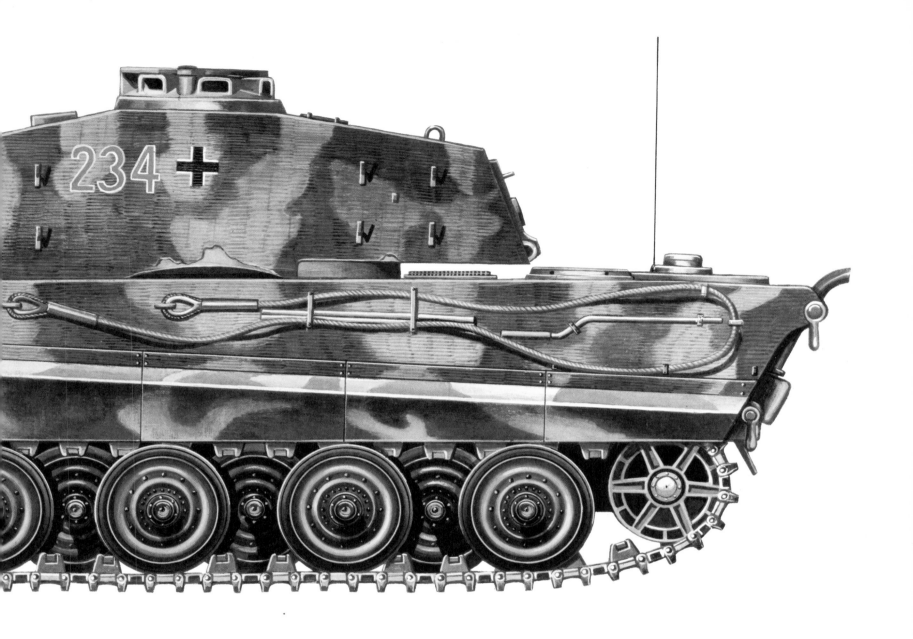

Tank VI, Tiger II Königstiger   (Germany)
(Sd. Kfz. 182)

In 1943 the German armored troops were able to neutralize, at least in single combat, the Russian tanks with their Tiger Is and Panthers. They nevertheless felt the need for heavier and better vehicles. This need was supplied by the Tiger II or "Königstiger" (Royal Tiger), which weighed 68 tons in battle trim and was therefore the heaviest tank to fight in World War II. Its 88-mm cannon could penetrate 4-inch armor plating at a range of about 1,100 yards, making it the most powerful tank in the field. However, by March 1945 only 485 tanks of this type were ready for action and consequently the new "wonder weapon" could not do much good. Actually, the tank designers of that day had far more ambitious plans: they had in mind an E 100 weighing 137 tons and a "Mouse" of 189 tons, but those monsters never reached the production stage.

Weight	74.8 short tons, 66.8 long tons (68 tons)
Length	33 ft. 9 in. (10.28 m) (including gun)
Width.	12 ft. 3 ½ in. (3.75 m)
Height	10 ft. 2 in. (3.1 m)
Engine	Maybach HL 230 P 30, 12-cylinder, watercooled, 600–700 h.p., 3,000 r.p.m.
Speed.	26 m.p.h. (42 km.p.h.)
Tank capacity. .	227.2 U.S. gal., 189.2 Imp. gal. (860 l)
Range.	74–106 miles (120–170 km)
Armament . . .	1 88 KwK 43 L/71, 2 mg
Ammunition . .	84 88-mm rds, 5,850 mg rds
Armor	150 mm, turret 185 mm
Crew	5
Number in series.	About 485
Year	1944–45

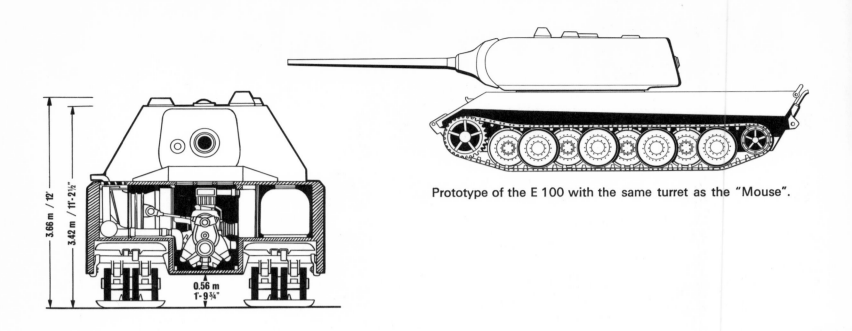

Prototype of the E 100 with the same turret as the "Mouse".

Whether as a forlorn hope or as a technical toy, Hitler commissioned the extravagantly heavy "Mouse" from Ferdinand Porsche in 1943 and two prototypes were built in the following year. The "Travelling Bunker" weighed 189 tons. The 1200-h.p. engine that drove the tracks through an electric transmission should have given the vehicle a top speed of 12 ½ m.p.h. Armament was a 128-mm cannon that fired 150-mm ammunition and recoiled about 3 feet. The shells weighed 120 or 155 pounds. The turret weighed about 50 tons, measured 10 feet across and its air-cooling system required 150 h.p. The "Mouse" could only be transported by rail on a special wagon. Since hardly any bridges could carry such a load it was designed to ford waterways up to 25 feet deep. No doubt other countries planned ultra-heavy combat vehicles, but the two prototypes of the "Mouse" were the heaviest to get beyond the drawing-board stage. They had just passed their first tests when they were blown up to prevent their capture by the advancing Russians.

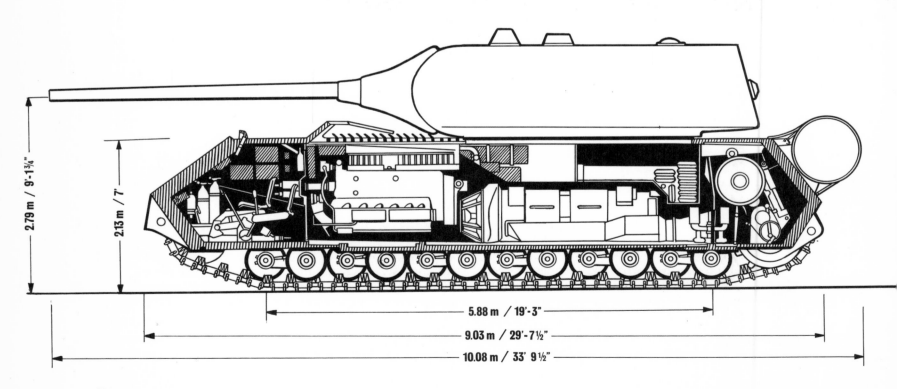

Modern Tanks 5

New tanks named after beasts of prey were expected to be the "wonder weapon" that would win the war at the eleventh hour. When events on the battlefield demolished the myth that lightning war was synonymous with lightning victory, Nazi propaganda cleverly exploited the fact that even in wartime German industry was capable of amazing performances in the design and production of modern weaponry. There is no doubt that in the early 1940s and still more towards the end of the war German-built tanks were technically as advanced as any of their contemporaries. But there is even less doubt that the industries of the Allied countries succeeded in constantly improving tank construction and, more important still, in delivering tanks in far greater numbers on the field of battle than war-worn Germany could ever hope to do. In the so-called Russian campaign the German army discovered that the vast spaces for which the tank was best suited could also prove fatal to it.

At the start of that campaign battles of encirclement marked the German advance. As a rule they ended with the total destruction of the enemy *matériel*. In fact, during these months the Red Army lost virtually all its light tanks. Subsequently, the battles of encirclement developed into battles of extermination and attrition. The German armored units often succeeded in breaking through a series of antitank blocks, penetrating to a depth of 20 miles, and rallying at a given spot almost undisturbed. But when after the breakthrough 3 undamaged tanks were all that remained of an entire regiment, the obvious question arose: which side had really won?

Soon the Red Army evolved what the German soldiers called "Panje-Taktik" ("Panje" was the name given to the Russians and the Poles). It consisted in small Soviet units driving in Panje sleighs behind the German front and attacking the tank divisions' "soft underbelly", causing such havoc that the advancing troops were forced to fall back. For the tank thrust or raid is only one side of the coin. The other, less showy and glorious side, is the sensitive but absolutely indispensable service organization.

Undoubtedly, tank servicing in the German army was very good, but there was no evading the laws of tank warfare. Of every hundred tanks one-third were engaged, one-third on the march and one-third under repair.

From the beginning of operations one could pinpoint a drawback of modern tank warfare: where an isolated soldier can take cover a tank unit can do so only quite inadequately or not at all. An interesting marginal observation in connection with tank warfare may be summed up in these words: armor plating grew stronger as morale declined. Each technical improvement in combat vehicles was soon followed by a similar technical improvement in antitank weapons. The only answer tank manufacturers could find to the increased efficiency of antitank guns was to strengthen the armor plating. But that, as was proved by searching tests on both sides, offered the crew very little additional protection. The attempt to give tanks stronger armor and as far as possible guns of greater range than a possible enemy's ended up inevitably by making the vehicles heavier and less mobile, with the result that what was gained on the roundabouts was lost on the swings. The only basis for the successful use of tanks might be summed up in the phrase: "A man with guts doesn't ask about the range of his gun; he drives close enough to the enemy to make sure of a hit."

In this connection, it is not insignificant that the German 37-mm antitank gun's slight penetrating power and almost total inefficacy against the Russian T34 tank earned it the nickname from the German soldiers of "Heeresanklopfgerät" (army doorknocker). In the French campaign of 1940 any successes chalked up by German antitank guns were due to the splendidly trained gunners, who managed to shoot straight into the ports of the French tanks.

(continued on page 133)

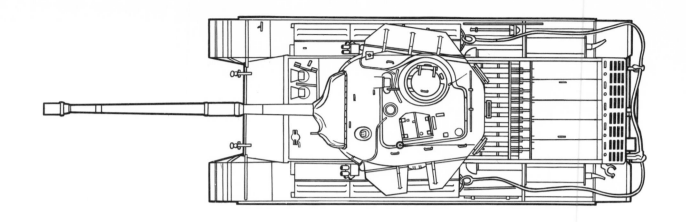

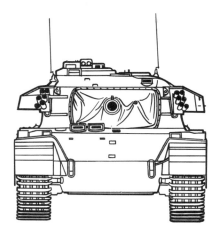

Though the heavy British Centurion was ordered in 1943 the war was decided long before it appeared in the field. The first six prototypes were despatched post haste to Germany in May 1945 but there was no need to engage them. Since then 21 versions of this tank have been built, but the first to see action was the Mark III; which served in Korea in January 1951. It is interesting to see how the Centurion's weight increased through the various stages of its development. The first was to have weighed about 40 tons but actually topped 42. The successive versions weighed about 47, then 49 and finally exceeded the 50-ton figure, which is critical for the Western European highway system. The weightiest version, the Centurion 5, appeared late in 1952. A feature of this tank is the steel side plating, which extends to the centre of the road wheels. During the war of June 1967 the Israeli troops painted such warlike inscriptions as "Suez Express" or "Tel Aviv-Cairo Daily" on the flanks of their Centurions. As a matter of fact, in good hands the veteran vehicle could get the better of the Soviet tanks, some of which were more modern and technically superior.

Main Battle Tank (FV.4011)   **(Great Britain)**
Centurion 5

Weight	62.6 short tons, 55.9 long tons (56.9 tons)
Length	32 ft. 3 in. (9.83 m) (including gun)
Width	11 ft. 1 in. (3.38 m)
Height	9 ft. 7 in. (2.91 m)
Engine	Meteor Mark 48, 12-cylinder, water-cooled, 650 h.p., 2,250 r.p.m.
Speed	21 m.p.h. (35 km.p.h.)
Tank capacity . .	145.4 U.S. gal., 121 Imp. gal. (550.3 l)
Range	65 miles (105 km)
Armament . . .	1 84 Ordnance QF 20-pdr Mark I, 2 mg, 12 smoke dischargers
Ammunition . .	64 20-pdr rds, 4,250 mg rds, 21 smoke candles, 12 signal flares
Armor	152 mm
Crew	4
Number in series .	Produced in large numbers
Year	1953

An Israeli Centurion V advancing during the war against Egypt in June 1967.

132

But technical innovations often failed to achieve the hoped-for improvement in the military situation; indeed they raised new difficulties and problems. During the legendary German advance on Kursk a special unit of 250 Tigers was formed. It suffered heavy losses. Later Panther units also suffered heavy losses caused by spontaneous combustion due to the low-powered engines, which were forced to run at exaggerated speed.

In spite of all this German soldiers never lost faith in the secret weapon. At the front German industry was credited with being capable of incredible performances. There were rumors of tanks made of new materials such as synthetic resin or bakelite. The hope that some day wonder tanks would roll off the assembly lines never died. As a matter of fact tanks were produced right up to the end of the war but they were not wonder tanks. They were delivered to the Western Allies, magnificently serviced and no less magnificently protected from air attack, in sufficient numbers to ensure final victory.

When did really modern tanks first put in an appearance? Experts could not possibly agree on the answer to that question. One may say, however, that the decisive breakthrough in the technical field occurred during the war, between 1943 and 1945. New materials, improved welding methods, far more efficient weaponry, more accurate optical equipment, more powerful engines and, last but not least, better communications between tank commanders by radio telephone—these are the features of the modern tanks that all the belligerent nations produced more or less at the same time. A certain degree of standardization was also achieved, in the sense that a given component of one tank (for instance, the transmission gear) was used in tanks of different types. This made production cheaper and more rational. Further, in the 1940s tanks first ran off the assembly lines in large numbers. Production of the legendary Russian T34 reached up to 10,000 a year. In the United States too mass-production methods were applied to tank manufacture and output of the famous Sherman M4 totalled close to 60,000.

The truth of the phrase coined by Clausewitz, "War is the father of all things", was confirmed by tank makers during World War II. In an amazingly short time plans were drafted, factories were built for realizing those plans, and within a few months a tank passed from the drawing-board to the battlefield. If we consider that today, despite immense technological advances, it takes ten years to develop a tank up to the mass-production stage, we must take our hats off to the achievements of those wartime constructors.

But even during the 1940s a great many designs ended up in the wastepaper basket. For instance, the Germans planned an ultraheavy machine weighing 189 tons in fighting trim. It was commissioned by Hitler in person in 1943 and two prototypes were built the following year. If the truth be told this steel monster, powered by a 1200 hp engine, was little more than a forlorn hope. For though its 128-mm cannon gave it enormous fire power its armor plating would have afforded but slight protection to the crew because the armor-piercing shells then available made steel plates simply a bad joke. Both sides adopted the view almost at the same time that salvation must be sought only in mobility and, where possible, in superior fire power. As a result tanks were made lighter and therefore more mobile, and armed with more powerful guns.

Great store was set on the element of surprise, which was sought in different ways by the various belligerent countries. The most obvious problem was that of making tanks capable of navigating waterways. It soon appeared that there were only two methods of doing that. Either the vehicle must be truly amphibious or it must be equipped for fording even quite deep waters. A Red Army propaganda film showed the solution which is still preferred by the Russians. Their tanks were prepared for crossing rivers by fitting a chimney-like schnorkel through which air was sucked into the hull. On reaching the opposite bank the schnorkel was discarded and the tank could virtually drive out of the water and into battle. In 1940 the German troops had schnorkel tanks prepared for the invasion of England and on June 22, 1941 they used them in Russia in order to cross the Bug. Makeshift arrangements of this kind were not altogether satisfactory, but the solution to the problem was not abandoned and tanks with amphibious capacity can today be found in France (AMX 30) and in Germany (Leopard).

An idea first developed by the American motorcar maker J. Walter Christie in the early 1920s was brought up again during the war. What Christie wanted was a tank that could fly, but the 7-ton winged vehicle with an 800 hp engine he built in the thirties never succeeded in leaving the ground. Nor were better results obtained during the war, at least under that form. In June 1945 the Americans transported by air the "General Chaffe" M24 light tank after it had been dismantled in an aircraft. However, under these conditions air transport brought no tactical advantage for it took the crew half a day to reassemble the vehicle after landing. Delivery by air of an M24 ready for action did not become a practical proposition until the introduction of the four-engine Globemaster transport plane.

It was also with an eye to transport by air, in other words for normal loading and unloading on board an aircraft, that the French built their AMX 13, a light tank that weighed only 13 tons. Today that vehicle can be carried by almost any medium or heavy transport plane.

(continued on page 159)

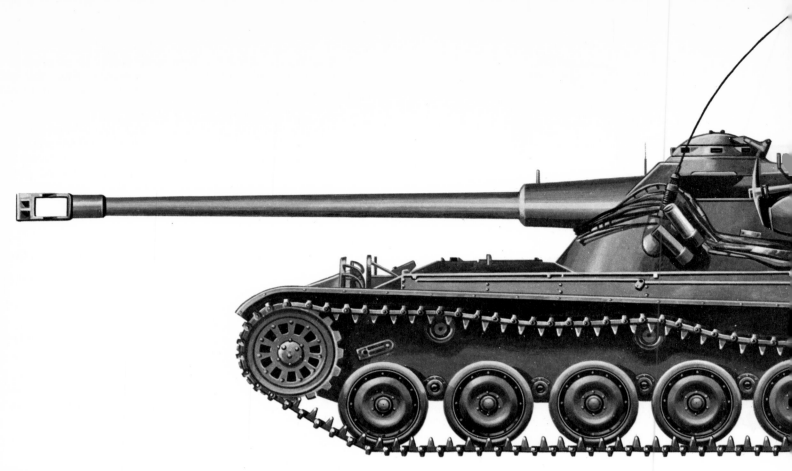

The Patton M47 **(right)** (named after the famous American tank general) was the first tank built in the United States after World War II. During that war and even more after the experience gained in the Korean War of the early fifties, when the Americans had only their M42 to put in the field, there was a call for a mass-produced standard tank. The M47 derived from the M46 but its turret incorporated some important innovations and its sighting instruments were better. The relatively heavy vehicle was delivered to the American army in 1952 and a little later to several allied countries, particularly NATO members, some of whom still use it.

Tank, M47 Patton   (U.S.A.)

Weight	48.6 short tons, 43.3 long tons (44 tons)
Length	27 ft. 11 in. (8.51 m)
Width	11 ft. 6 ¼ in. (3.51 m)
Height	10 ft. 11 in. (3.33 m)
Engine	Continental AV-1790-5, 58.7 or 7B, 12-cylinder, 810 h.p., 2,800 r.p.m.
Speed	37 m.p.h. (60 km.p.h.)
Tank capacity . .	233 U.S. gal., 194 Imp. gal. (882 l)
Range	100 miles (161 km)
Armament . . .	1 90-mm cannon T.119 L 40.9, later T.119 E1 (M.36) L/43, 3 mg
Ammunition . .	71 cannon rds, 3,440 mg rds, later 11,500 rds
Armor	75–100 mm, turret 115 mm
Crew	5
Number in series .	Produced in large numbers
Year	1950

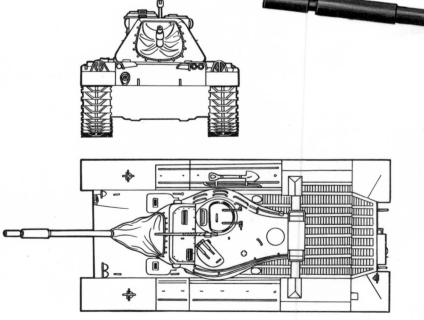

134

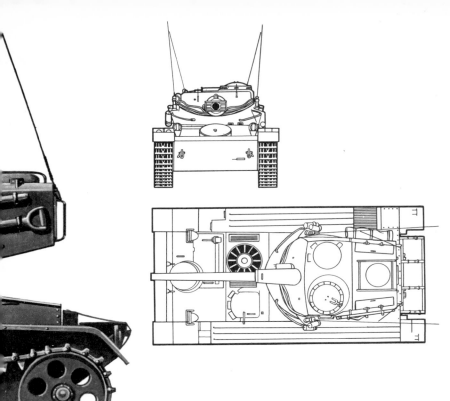

The French AMX 13 light tank **(left)** is proof that tank designers can learn from their mistakes. After the end of World War II the French presented their new 50-ton AMX 50 but it proved too costly for mass production. When in 1949 the same makers presented another AMX tank that weighed less than 15 tons, it caused a minor technical sensation. The engine of what had been designed as a reconnaissance and pursuit vehicle was located left front and the driver sat alongside the engine compartment. The gun loader's job was done by an automatic loading device that functioned reliably independent of the position of the turret.

Light Tank, AMX 13 Model 51   (France)

Weight	16.3 short tons, 14.6 long tons (14.8 tons)
Length	20 ft. 9 in. (6.33 m)
Width	8 ft. 3 in. (2.51 m)
Height	7 ft. 2 in. (2.18 m)
Engine	SOFAM 8 Gxb, 8-cylinder, watercooled, 270 h.p., 3,200 r.p.m.
Speed	37 m.p.h. (60 km.p.h.)
Armament . . .	1 75-mm SA cannon, model 50, 1 mg model 1931E, 4 smoke bomb projectors
Ammunition . .	37 cannon rds, 1,500 mg rds, 12 smoke bombs
Armor	40 mm
Crew	3
Year	1951

U.S.A. 30164251

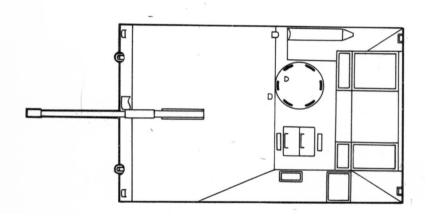

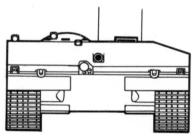

Tank, Stridsvagn Strv 103 "S"   **(Sweden)**
Prototype

Weight	40.7 short tons, 36.4 long tons (37 tons)
Length	28 ft. 10 ½ in. (8.8 m)
Width	10 ft. 10 in. (3.3 m)
Height	7 ft. 8 in. (2.34 m)
Engine	Rolls-Royce K 60 with extra gas turbine, multi-fuel engine, 240–330 h.p.
Speed	31 m.p.h. (50 km.p.h.)
Armament . . .	1 105-mm cannon K 105, 1 anti-aircraft mg 7.62 mm, 2 mg
Crew	3
Number in series .	Prototype
Year	1963

After World War II most tank designers in both east and west kept to the traditional silhouette with track, hull and turret. The Swedes however built an entirely new armored vehicle in the sixties. The Strv 103 S "Stridsvagn" (Combat Car) has no turret. Its 105-mm cannon is aimed hydraulically and by the vehicle's own movement. The front and rear wheels can be adjusted hydraulically to give the track the requisite tension. The Swedish tank is designed with an eye to the future: it offers its three-man crew all the protection against atomic, biological and chemical weapons feasible today.

136

The Leopard, the first tank built in Germany after the war, has been supplied to several NATO countries.

The Leopard was designed for action in Central Europe.

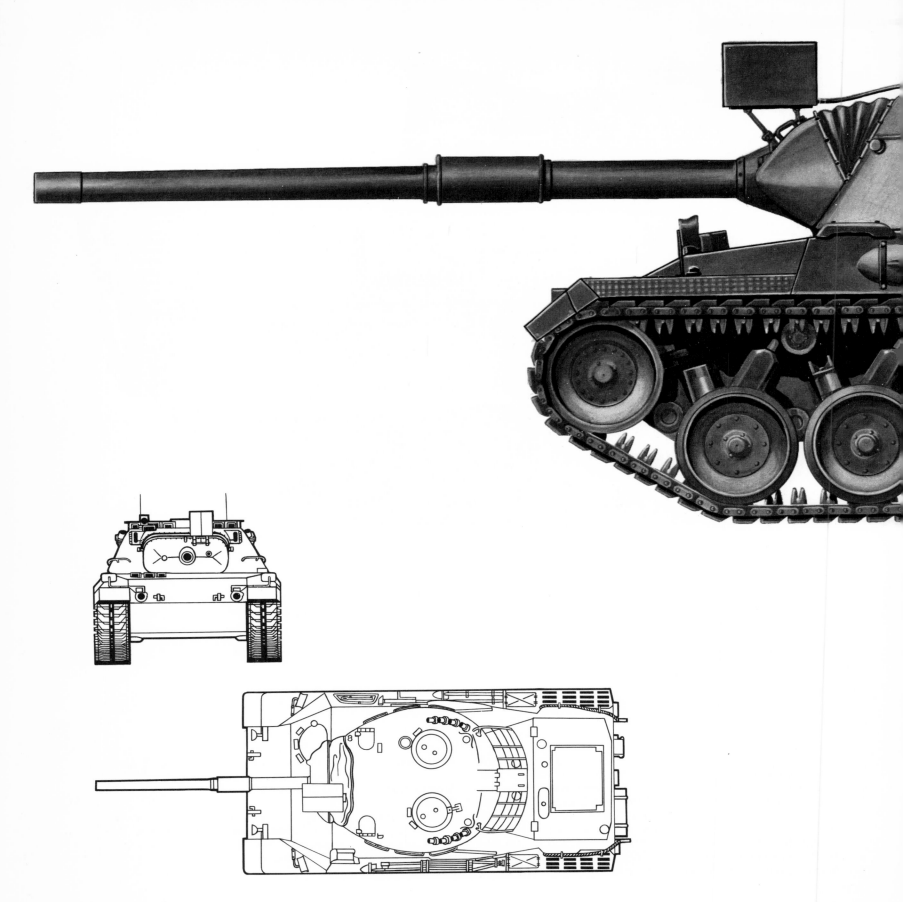

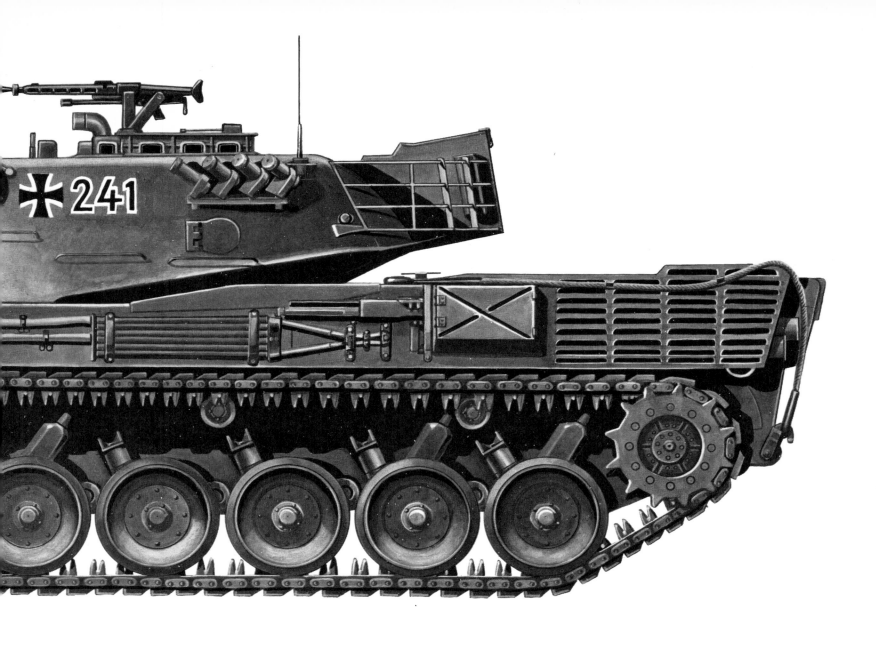

When the Federal Republic of Germany became a member of NATO with an army of its own, the French, Italians and Germans agreed to develop a standard tank specially suited to their needs. From 1957 to 1961 the three Defense Ministries and two groups of manufacturers busied themselves with the project. After one of the groups had withdrawn and the French had built their AMX 30 the Munich firm of Krauss-Maffei was commissioned to build a new German tank. The first Leopard rolled off the assembly line in September 1966.

Main Battle Tank, Leopard Series 2   (Germany)

Weight	44 short tons, 39.3 long tons (40 tons)
Length	31 ft. 3 ½ in. (9.54 m)
Width	10 ft. 8 in. (3.25 m)
Height	7 ft. 11 in. (2.4 m)
Engine	Daimler-Benz MB 838, 10-cylinder, watercooled, 830 h.p., 2,200 r.p.m. Supercharged
Speed	40 m.p.h. (65 km.p.h.)
Range	About 373 miles (600 km)
Armament . . .	1 105 KL7A3, 2 7.6-mm mg, 8 smoke dischargers
Ammunition . .	60 105-mm rds
Crew	4
Number in series .	Produced in large numbers. Up until May 1969 some 1,950 models were delivered, the later series with slight modifications.
Year	1966

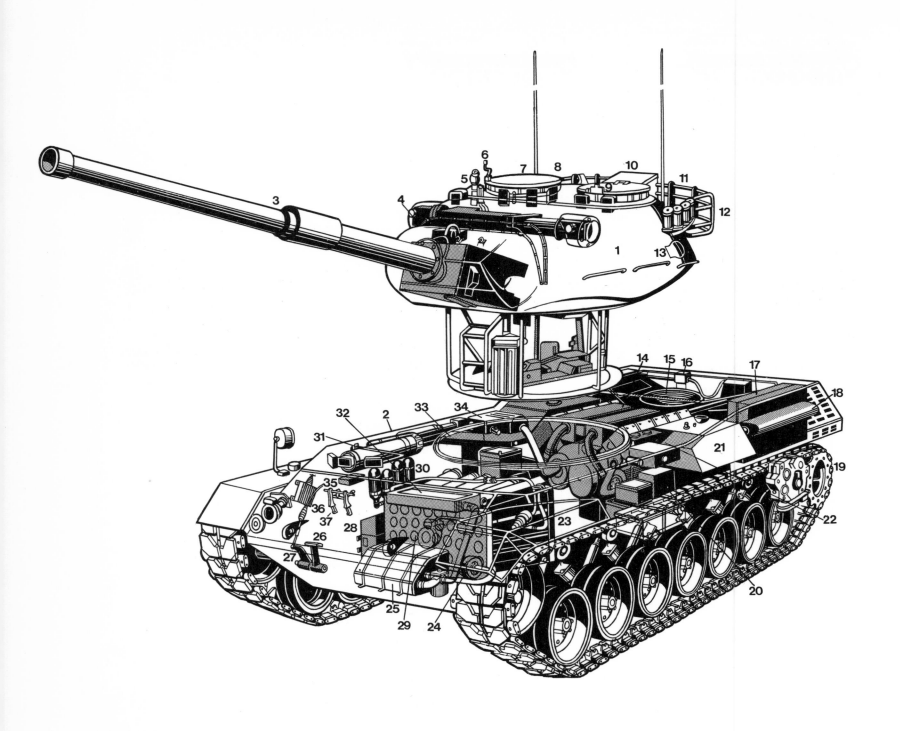

1, turret; 2, hull; 3, 105-mm cannon; 4, rangefinder; 5, pancratic panoramic sighting telescope; 6, mount for anti-aircraft machine gun; 7, commander's hatch; 8, goniometer; 9, loader's hatch; 10, infrared sighting searchlight; 11, rear storage rack; 12, smoke-bomb thrower; 13, ammunition port; 14, engine; 15, ventilator; 16, braking system; 17, radiator; 18, silencer; 19, driving wheel; 20, accumulators; 21, fuel tank; 22, fuel containers; 23, suction nozzles (ventilation and ABC protection systems); 24, main nozzle (ventilation and ABC protection systems); 25, air filter (ventilation and ABC protection systems); 26, brake pedal; 27, accelerator; 28, instrument panel; 29, magazine; 30, fire extinguishers; 31, coolant preheater and air-conditioning unit; 32, coarse dust filter (ventilation and ABC protection systems); 33, warm air system; 34, combustion air filter; 35, steering handle; 36, change-speed gear; 37, hand brake.

140

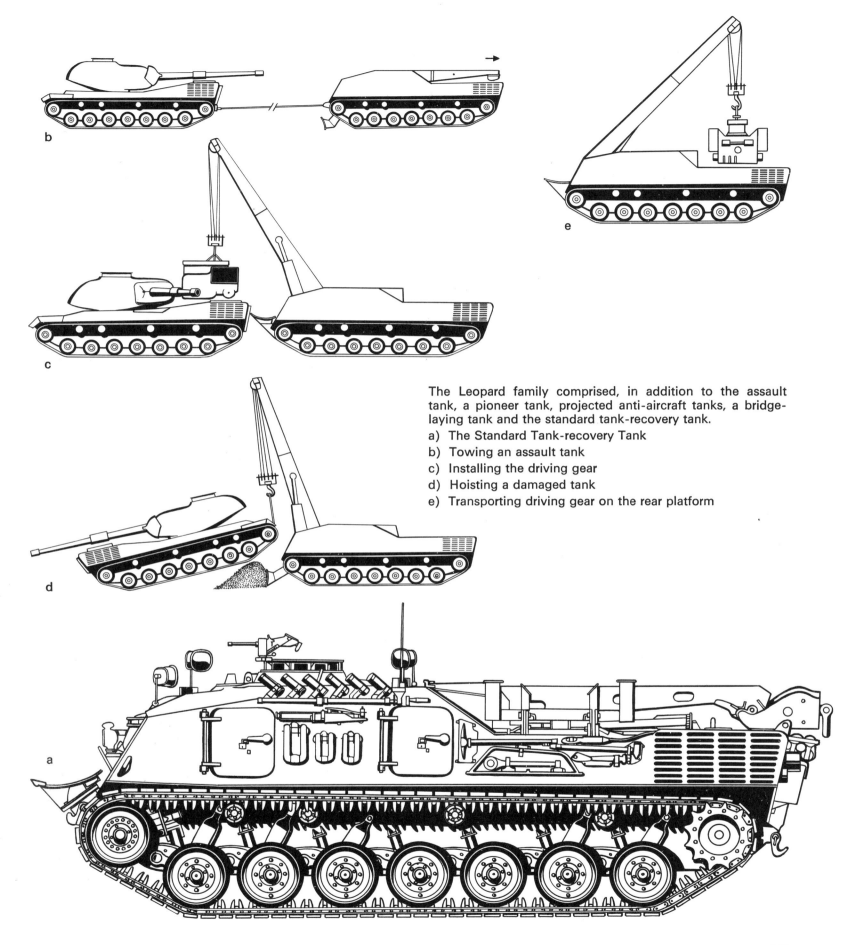

The Leopard family comprised, in addition to the assault tank, a pioneer tank, projected anti-aircraft tanks, a bridge-laying tank and the standard tank-recovery tank.

a) The Standard Tank-recovery Tank
b) Towing an assault tank
c) Installing the driving gear
d) Hoisting a damaged tank
e) Transporting driving gear on the rear platform

141

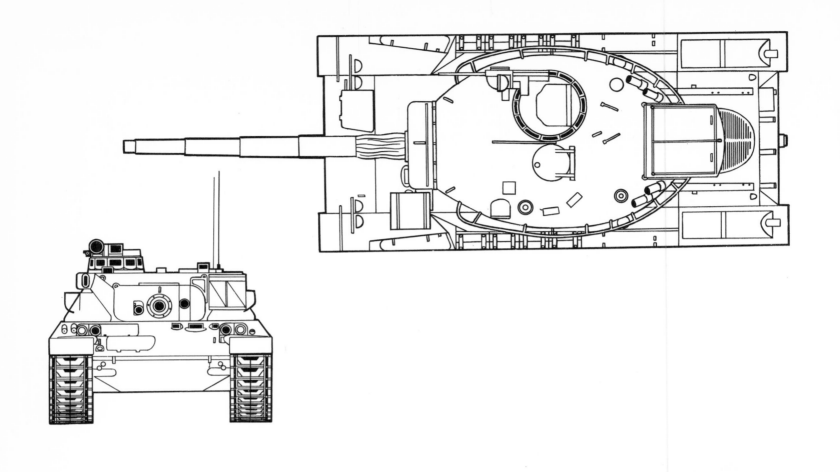

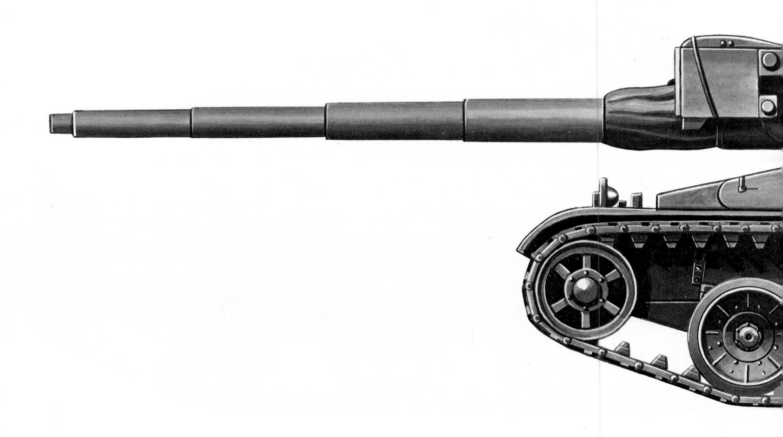

142

The French AMX 30 battle tank was the outcome of joint studies by France, Germany and Italy, all three NATO members. But the ambitious and certainly idealistic project of a Western European NATO standard tank came to nothing. While the development of the German Leopard took its course, the French brought out the relatively light AMX 30 (named after the Atelier de Construction d'Issy-les-Moulineaux). The 720-h.p. multi-fuel engine gives the 36-ton vehicle a good turn of speed. It also has extraordinary fording capability and, like most new models, is equipped with an ABC protection system. The commander's dome is the only bulge on its very flat profile. The AMX 30 is now the main weapon of the French armed forces.

Tank, AMX 30 (France)

Weight	39.6 short tons, 35.4 long tons (36 tons)
Length	31 ft. 2 in. (9.5 m)
Width	10 ft. 2 in. (3.1 m)
Height	9 ft. 4 in. (2.85 m)
Engine	Hispano-Suiza H.S. 110, diesel, 720 h.p., 2,600 r.p.m.
Speed	22–25 m.p.h. (35–40 km.p.h.)
Range	305–373 miles (500–600 km)
Armament	1 105-mm cannon DEFA D 1511, 2 mg, 4 smoke dischargers
Armor	50 mm
Crew	4
Number in series	In production 1967–69
Year	1962–67

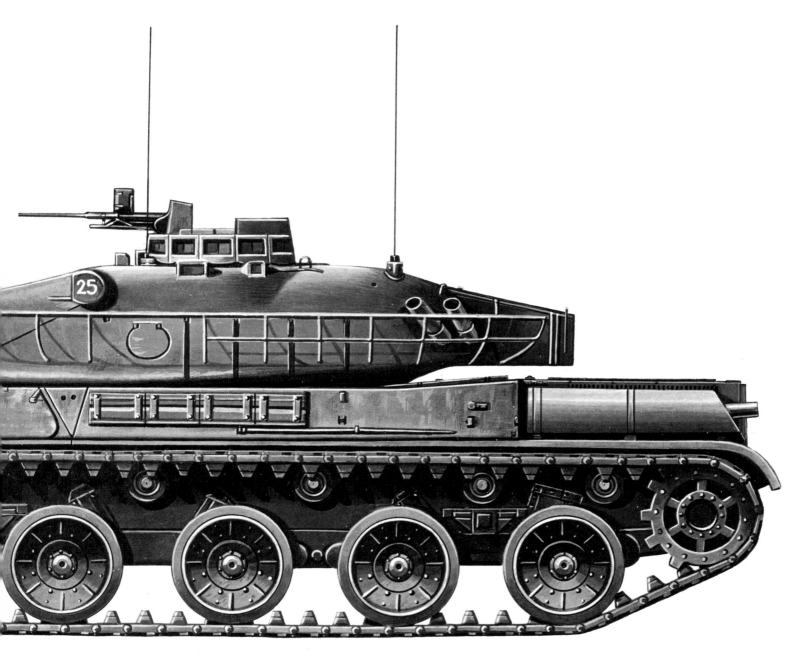

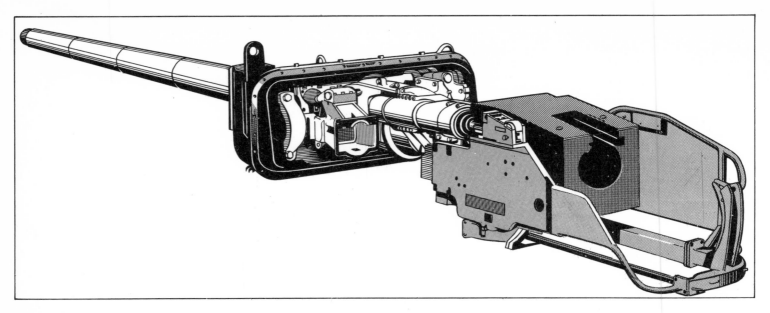

The AMX 30's semi-automatic 105-mm cannon.

The AMX 30's infrared sighting searchlight.

Front view of a French AMX 30.

The French AMX 30 was developed alongside the German Leopard but weighs a good deal less than its rival.

144

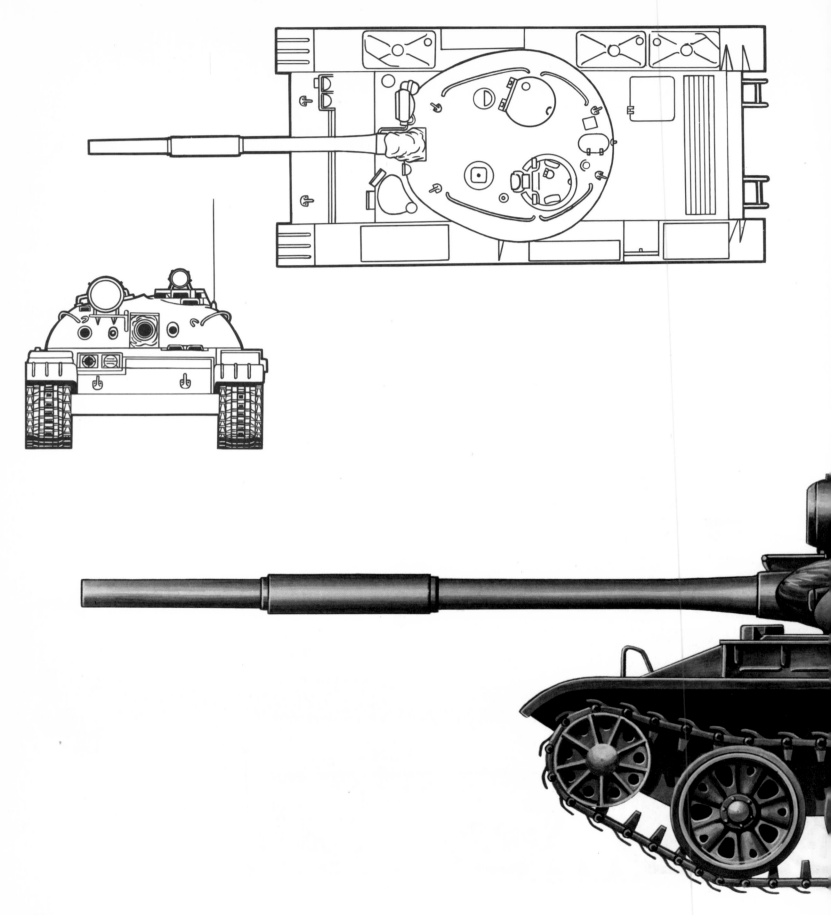

Tank T62   (U.S.S.R.)

Weight	40.7–45.2 short tons, 36.4–40.35 long tons (37–41 tons)
Length	30 ft. 10 in. with cannon (9.4 m)
Width	11 ft. 1 in. (3.37 m)
Height	7 ft. 4 ½ in. (2.25 m)
Engine	580 h.p.
Armament . . .	1 115-mm cannon, 1 7.62-mm mg
Crew	4
Number in series .	Produced in large numbers
Year	from 1965

The Russian T62 battle tank is far from being revolutionary or even new: many of its structural features were taken over from the T34 and T54/55; the drive and track mechanism in particular are practically unchanged. It has, however, an extremely efficient 115-mm cannon with considerably longer range and firing accuracy than other Soviet tanks. The 37-ton vehicle is not outstandingly mobile, but has far better fording and submersion capability than western tanks of the same generation, so that watercourses are no great obstacle for it. The flat, tortoise-shaped T62, first delivered to the Soviet army in 1965, is somewhat lower than the Leopard and AMX 30, which date from about the same year.

147

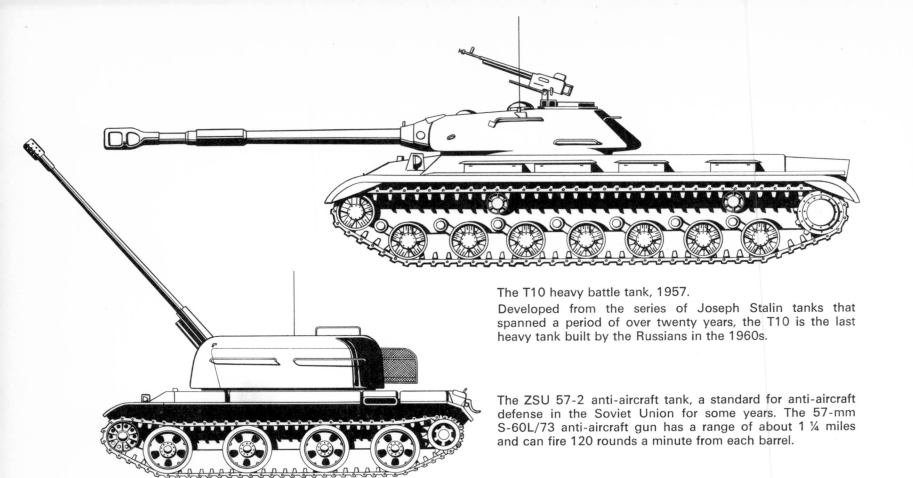

The T10 heavy battle tank, 1957.
Developed from the series of Joseph Stalin tanks that spanned a period of over twenty years, the T10 is the last heavy tank built by the Russians in the 1960s.

The ZSU 57-2 anti-aircraft tank, a standard for anti-aircraft defense in the Soviet Union for some years. The 57-mm S-60L/73 anti-aircraft gun has a range of about 1 ¼ miles and can fire 120 rounds a minute from each barrel.

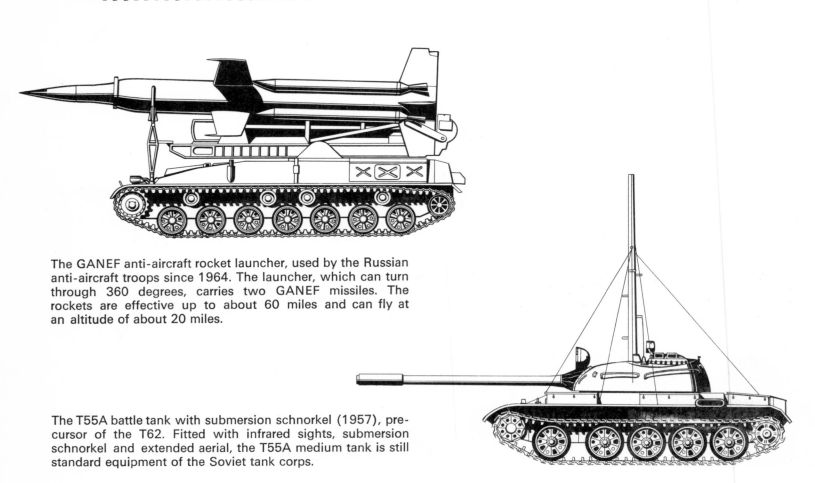

The GANEF anti-aircraft rocket launcher, used by the Russian anti-aircraft troops since 1964. The launcher, which can turn through 360 degrees, carries two GANEF missiles. The rockets are effective up to about 60 miles and can fly at an altitude of about 20 miles.

The T55A battle tank with submersion schnorkel (1957), precursor of the T62. Fitted with infrared sights, submersion schnorkel and extended aerial, the T55A medium tank is still standard equipment of the Soviet tank corps.

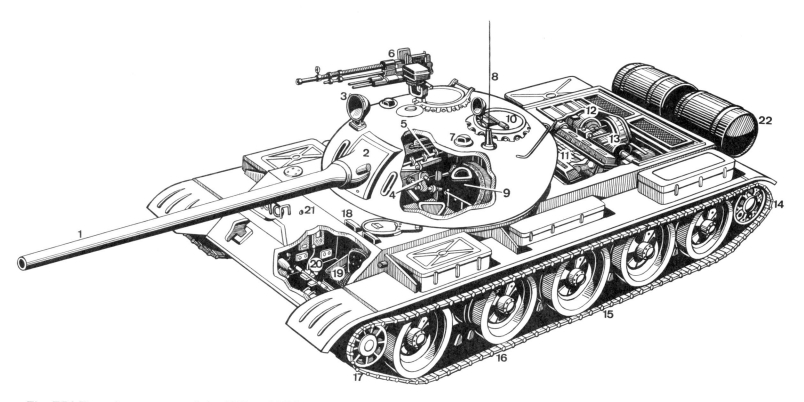

The T54 Type A, precursor of the T55 and T62

1, 100-mm cannon without bore evacuation; 2, screen; 3, infrared searchlight; 4, elevating gear; 5, turret telescopic sight; 6, 12.7-mm anti-aircraft machine gun; 7, gunner's telescopic sight; 8, aerial; 9, commander's seat; 10, commander's dome; 11, W2 12-cylinder diesel engine; 12, planetary gear; 13, gearbox; 14, driving wheel; 15, track; 16, free wheels; 17, guide wheel; 18, driver's periscope; 19, driver's seat; 20, steering lever; 21, front machine gun.

The BTR-40 P (PTURS) "Sagger" rocket-launching pursuit tank has been developed from the BTR-40 reconnaissance car since 1962. The launching platform, which can be lowered, carries six "Sagger" antitank rockets. The 6-ton vehicle is very fast and mobile; the small wheels in the middle can be extended or retracted to suit the terrain.

Soviet manoeuvres with troops of various arms. Russian BTR 60 troop-carriers with tank support attack a wood.

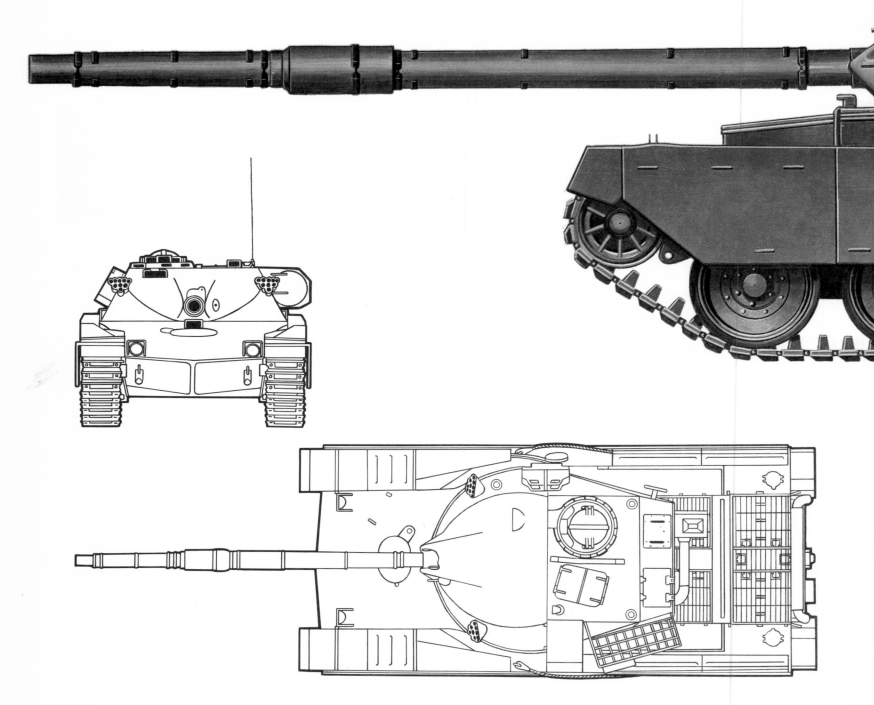

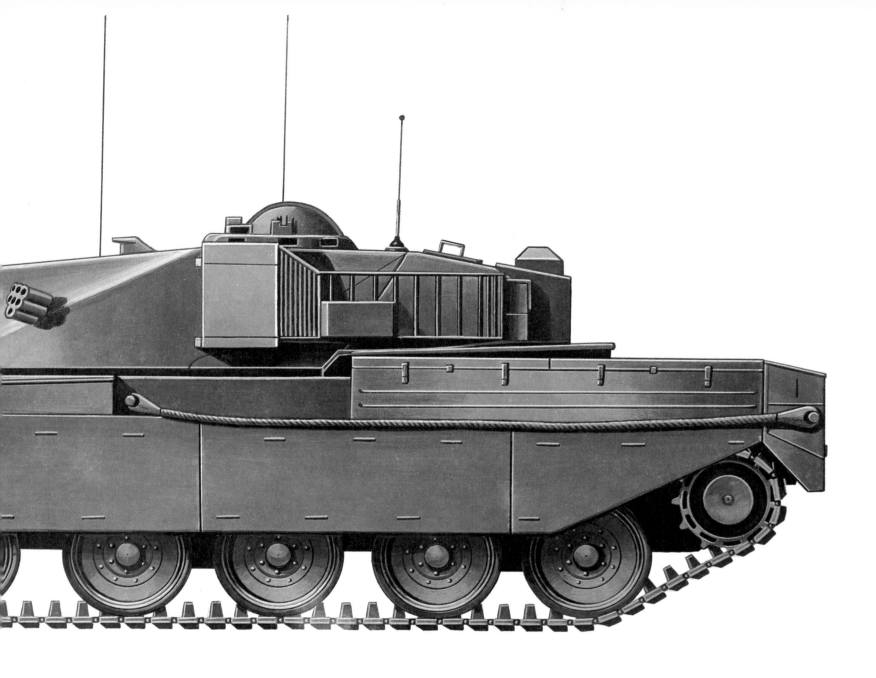

Tank (F.V. 4201) Chieftain   (Great Britain)

Weight	56.6 short tons, 50.6 long tons (51.4 tons)
Length	36 ft. 4 ½ in. (11.09 m)
Width	11 ft. 5 ¾ in. (3.5 m)
Height . . .	9 ft. (2.75 m)
Engine	Leyland L.60 diesel, 6-cylinder, 700 h.p., 2,400 r.p.m.
Speed	25 m.p.h. (40 km.p.h.)
Range	240 miles (387 km)
Armament . . .	1 120-mm cannon ROF, 3 mg, 18 smoke dischargers
Armor	120 mm, turret 150 mm
Year	In production from 1967

When the British decided to find a successor to their Centurion and Conqueror, they chose the Chieftain. Though it should have been ready in 1965, mass production did not get under way until two years later. And then not only was it unable to perform its task satisfactorily but it also failed to fulfil the hopes that it would be a good export article. The Americans considered the Chieftain the best tank built in Europe since the war but, although at some £100,000, it cost about the same as the German Leopard, it found fewer foreign buyers. Equipped with a 120-mm cannon and a 12.7-mm one-shot machine gun, the Chieftain weighs about 51 tons and is therefore inevitably more cumbersome than its lighter rivals, which weigh between 30 and 40 tons and have a better chance of selling on the Continent.

With its 51 tons the technically advanced British Chieftain
oversteps the weight limit for operations on the European
Continent. Nonetheless, it has boosted the fighting strength
of the British troops in Germany.

154

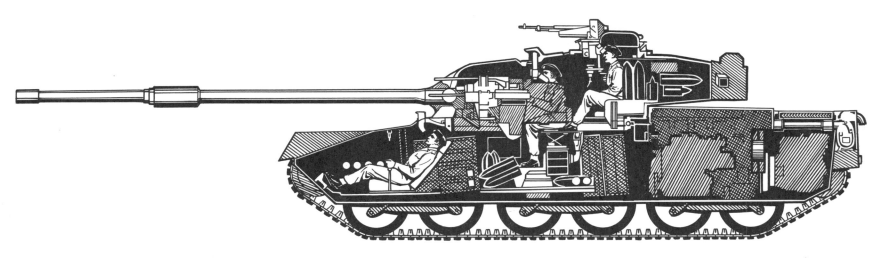

Cross-section of the Chieftain. The commander, gunner and driver (in reclining position) are shown; the radio operator-cum-loader has been omitted for clarity's sake.

Observation, Sighting and Laying Equipment on Chieftain
1, 120-mm cannon cradle; 2, gunner's telescopic sight; 3, gunner's periscope; 4, cowl with wiper; 5, 7.62-mm machine gun; 6, commander's elevating gear; 7, periscope wiper; 8, infrared searchlight; 9, commander's revolving dome; 10, periscope for 9; 11, dome rotating gear; 12, dome reversing gear; 13, commander's binocular telescope; 14, commander's collimator; 15, pump and rod, temperature-compensated; 16, gunner's clinometer.

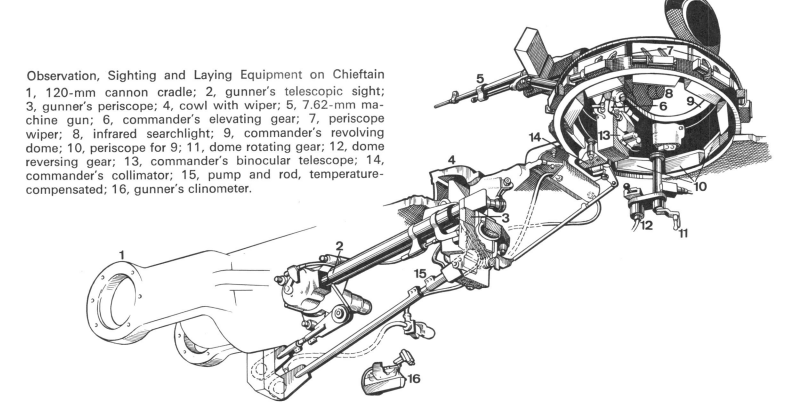

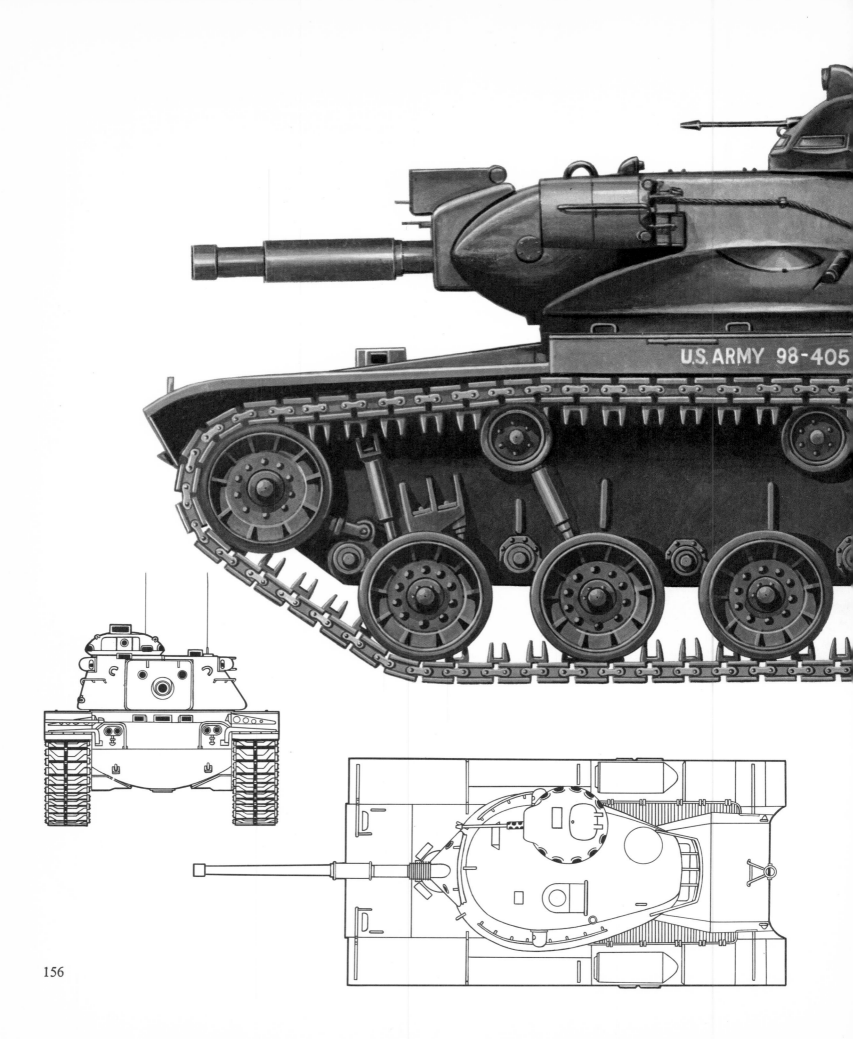

U.S. ARMY 98-405

156

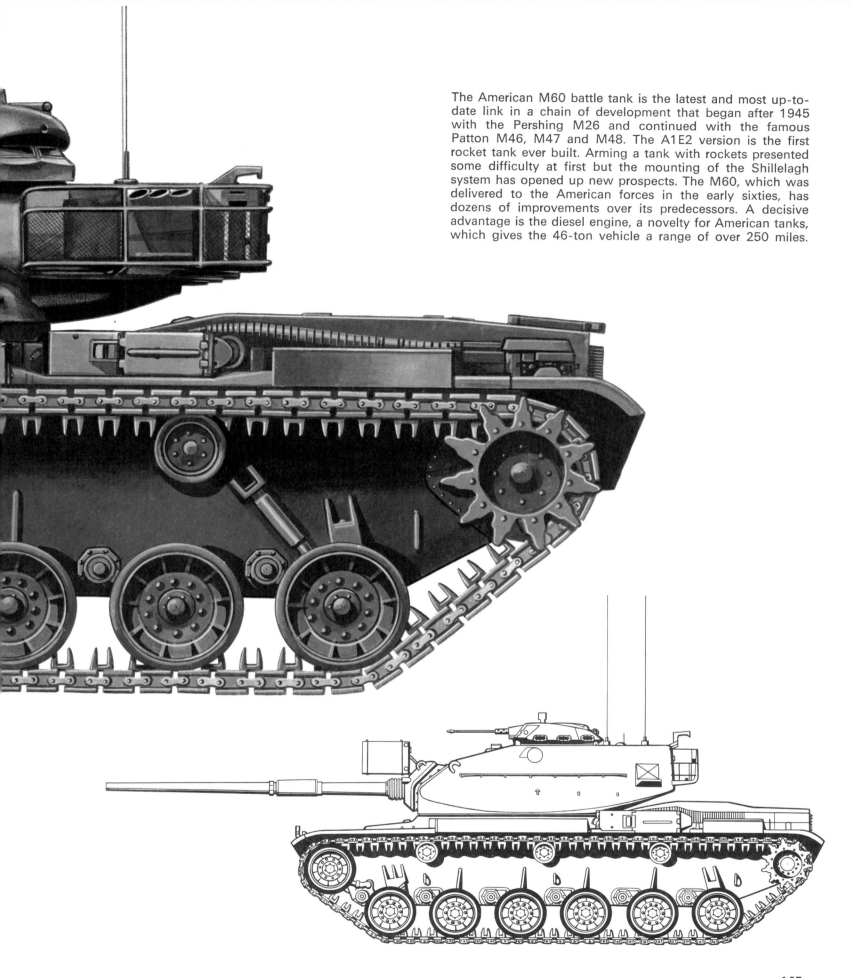

The American M60 battle tank is the latest and most up-to-date link in a chain of development that began after 1945 with the Pershing M26 and continued with the famous Patton M46, M47 and M48. The A1E2 version is the first rocket tank ever built. Arming a tank with rockets presented some difficulty at first but the mounting of the Shillelagh system has opened up new prospects. The M60, which was delivered to the American forces in the early sixties, has dozens of improvements over its predecessors. A decisive advantage is the diesel engine, a novelty for American tanks, which gives the 46-ton vehicle a range of over 250 miles.

The first tank equipped for shooting down aircraft: the American M60 with the Shillelagh rocket launcher.

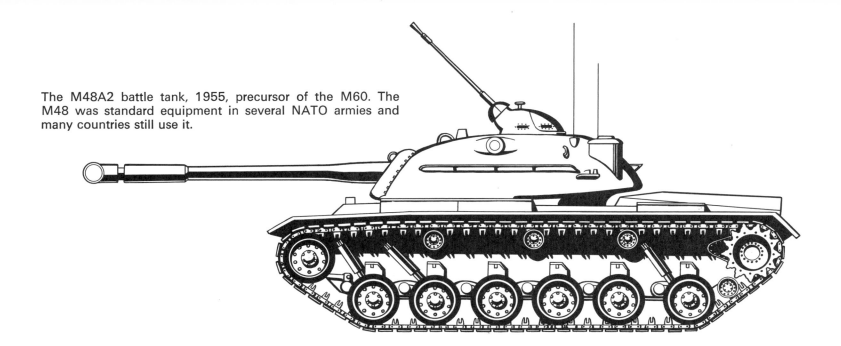

The M48A2 battle tank, 1955, precursor of the M60. The M48 was standard equipment in several NATO armies and many countries still use it.

Plenty of the large, powerful aircraft that can drop guns are specially designed for that purpose. The Soviet Union has the ASU 57, a fast, lightly armored vehicle with open cockpit and a 57-mm gun. It can be dropped firmly fixed on a spring-loaded platform, float to the ground under clustered parachutes, and be made ready for battle in next to no time.

Since 1945 the armed forces of the two military alliances, the North Atlantic Treaty Organization and the Warsaw Pact, have been equipped with "modern" tanks. In the east the Soviet Union, largely owing to its great experience in tank construction, enjoys a monopoly. In the west, despite nationalistic notions of competition and prestige, there has been a certain amount of co-operation. An example of this is the German Leopard, which is the outcome of collaboration between Germany and France, though halfway through the planning stage the two countries agreed to disagree and each went his own way. The Germans developed and built the Leopard; the French their AMX 30. The British Chieftain instead was a purely national affair and there were high hopes of selling it abroad; but they failed to materialize owing to the "market situation" and the military circumstances.

The original joint German-American project for a main battle tank came to nought owing to divergent views as to the purpose of the Type 70, as it was called. Since then there has been some talk of the possible joint development of a German-British tank. According to the experts, it would incorporate the best features of the British 52-ton Chieftain and the German 39-ton Leopard and be fitted with the very latest in electronic equipment. This "synthesis in steel" should begin to come off the assembly line in the early 1980s.

The appearance of new arms, notably wire-guided weapons and atomic tactical missiles, have had considerable influence on the present-day conception of the tank. Guided on its trajectory by the gunner—and that with very great precision—the wire-guided missile has a range equivalent to that of the heaviest tank cannon. The penetrating power of its hollow-charge warhead is as much as 300 mm, which is more than double the thickest armor that can protect a tank. These simple missiles can be used by infantry, tank corps and even airborne troops. The modern tank has abandoned the theory of *absolute* protection and has had to make do with the relative protection obtained by a combination of armor, reduction of silhouette and better profile. This compromise has led to the development of tanks armed with a 100–115-mm guns and weighing between 35 and 40 tons, instead of the 47 tons of the World War II Panther with its 75-mm cannon. Examples include the Swiss Pz 61, the German Leopard, the French AMX 30 and the Soviet Union's T54, T55 and T62. These machines have engines that develop between 15 and 20 hp to the ton, thus assuring them great mobility which increases their protection.

In this respect the only exception is the British Chieftain (51 tons, 120-mm cannon, 25 mph) but it has not found a foreign purchaser whereas the Leopard has attracted customers in Belgium, the Netherlands, Denmark, Italy and Spain. The American M60 represents an intermediate size between these two tanks which are now generically known as "battle tanks".

Will the appearance of nuclear weapons on the battlefield render armored weapons obsolete, just as artillery rendered the medieval cavalry obsolete? There has been no sign of this yet, not because the military are essentially

(continued on page 163)

159

The MBT 70 was to have replaced or supplemented the American M48 and M60 and the German Leopard in the early seventies. On August 1, 1963, the governments of the two countries agreed to develop and build the vehicle as a joint German-American project. The first important difference of opinion arose in connection with its armament. The Americans insisted on their Shillelagh missile system, whereas the Germans wanted to have the possibility of alternately mounting a high-power cannon, which has the advantage over a rocket system of being more effective up to a range of 2,200 yards. A final decision on this point was never reached. Both countries had already built six prototypes. The possibility of lowering hull and turret by means of a hydraulic device, thus bringing the vehicle down "on its knees", as it were, made a great impression in Germany. But mass production of the MBT 70 as a joint project never materialized and late in 1969 the committees of the two countries announced that the development of the tank had been terminated. The spokesman stated reassuringly that the money spent on it had not been thrown away for the results achieved in the preliminary stages of design and construction would be incorporated in the national tank programmes of the two countries. The joint development of the MBT 70 spread over six years and cost some 200 million dollars. So the 50-ton tank, without ever being engaged in battle, caused an explosion typical of present-day tank construction—namely a cost explosion.

Main Battle Tank, KPz 70 (MBT 70) (Germany/U.S.A.)

Weight	50.6 short tons, 45.2 long tons (46 tons)
Length	29 ft. 10 ½ in. (9.1 m)
Width	11 ft. 6 ½ in. (3.51 m)
Height	6 ft. 6 ½ in. lowered (1.99 m)
	7 ft. 6 in. normal (2.29 m)
Engine	Daimler-Benz MB-873, 12-cylinder, watercooled, supercharged, 1,500 h.p., 2,600 r.p.m.
	or:
	Continental, 12-cylinder, aircooled, 1,495 h.p., 2,800 r.p.m.
Speed	43 m.p.h. (70 km.p.h.) forwards or backwards
Range	404 miles (650 km)
Armament . . .	1 152-mm projector for Shillelagh missile and conventional ammunition
	or:
	1 120-mm automatic gun, 1 7.62-mm mg, smoke and high explosive mortar
Crew	3
Number in series .	Prototype
Year	1967–69

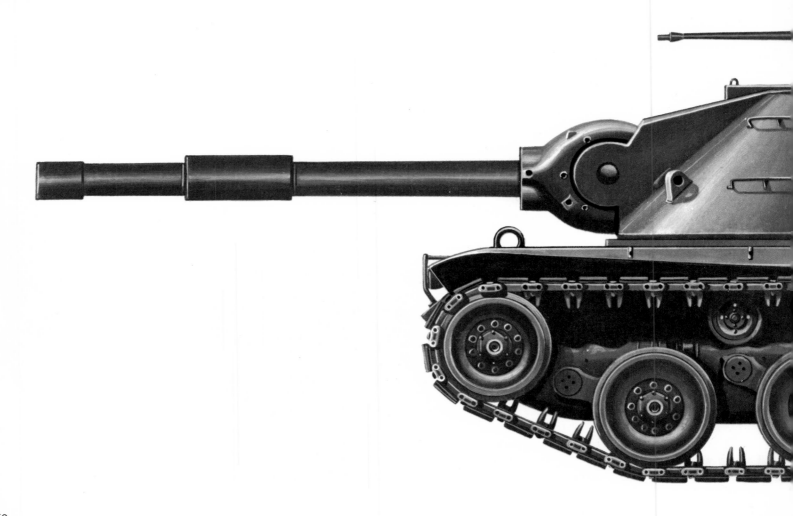

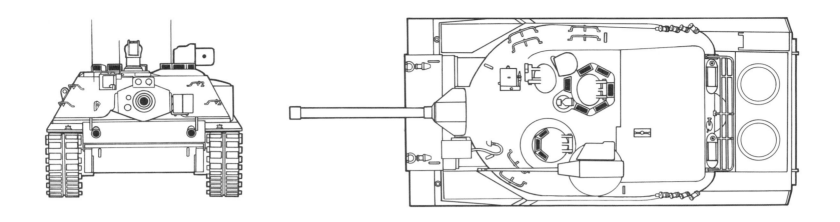

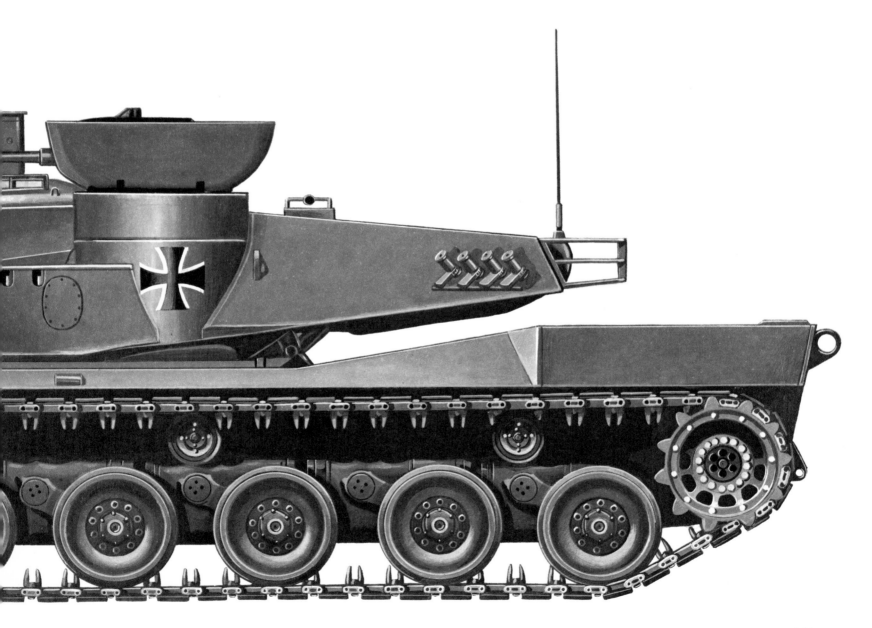

The German-American joint project for main battle tank 70 was dropped before production of the 70s started. Features of the vehicle will be incorporated in future developments.

162

conservative but because reflection and experience have led them to the following conclusions:

1) Armor of 25 mm and over provides the crew enclosed in the vehicle with sufficient protection against the effects of radiation for a long enough period for the tanks to be able either to take advantage of the breach created in the enemy ranks by the nuclear explosion or, in the case of defensive action, to close up.

2) Furthermore, in the midst of the devastation wrought by the use of an atomic tactical weapon, tracked armored vehicles would retain mobility and escape possibilities denied wheeled vehicles; the crews of the latter, if not armored, would in addition be exposed to the dangerous effects of nuclear radiation.

From 1942 on the Germans were preoccupied with putting infantry, artillery and assault engineers into armored halftracks but they lacked the means to complete this scheme. The Americans and British also failed to motorize and armor all their infantry by 1945, and the Russians were even farther behind.

The possibility of nuclear war, however, has accelerated the process in all the armies of the world, despite the considerable expense involved in the transition from motorized to armored tracked vehicles. Modern types of armored vehicles now include the following typical examples:

— armored personnel carriers like the M113 (US), most of them amphibians;
— anti-tank tanks (or tank destroyers) (AMX 13 French, SU85 and SU100 Soviet);
— light tanks equipped with 30, 35 and 57 mm recoilless rifles (Ontos);
— tracked artillery;
— carriers with launching ramps for atomic tactical missiles (US, USSR);
— bridge-carrying tanks;
— self-propelled vehicle ferries.

Thus is planned the creation of great, integrally mechanized units advancing in a block, deterred by no obstacle, at a pace which, according to the calculations of Soviet theoreticians, should allow them to cover about 63 miles a day for periods of several days!

Modern tanks must still meet the demands of the army, namely long-range action, maximum fire power, a large stock of ammunition, high-speed fire, adequate protection against low-flying aircraft, suitability for night fighting. For their part the manufacturers have not yet found a solution to the vicious circle engendered by contradictory requirements: great firing power, absolute protection, speed and mobility. In fact all tank design is perforce a more or less successful compromise.

163

COLOR ILLUSTRATIONS

COMPARATIVE CATALOG OF TYPES

SCALE 1 : 75

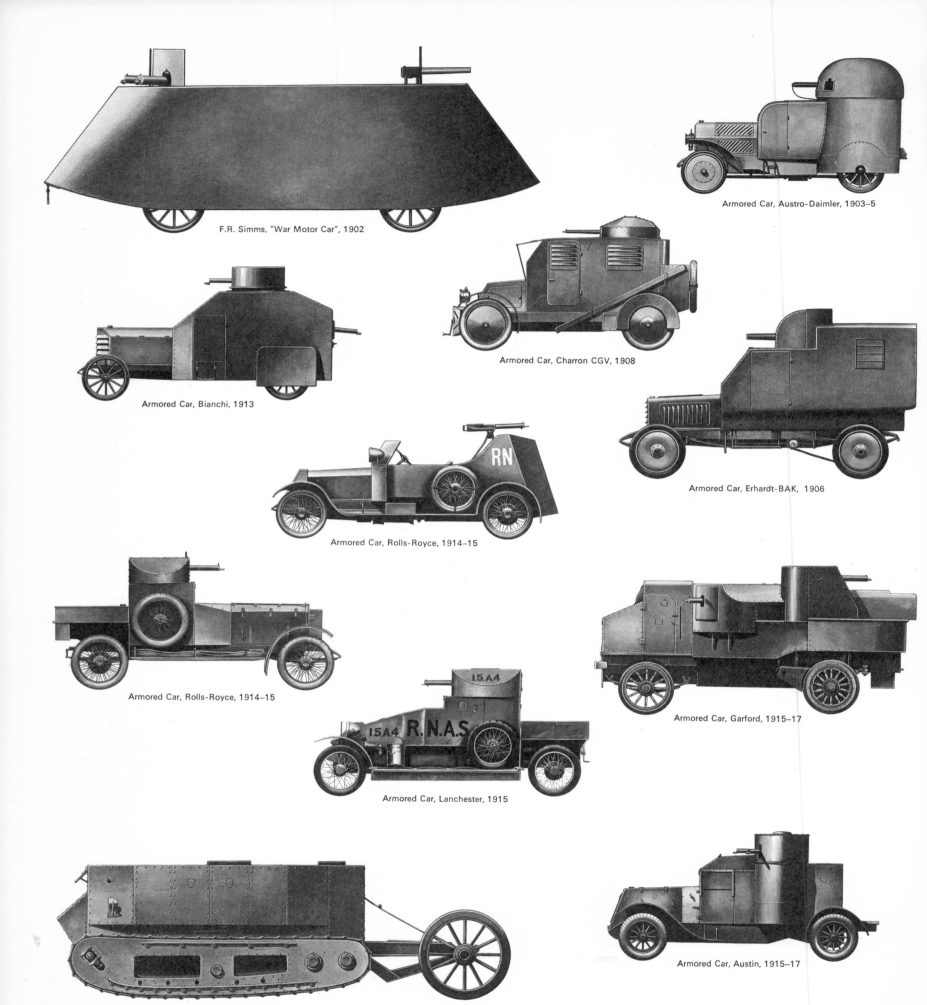

F.R. Simms, "War Motor Car", 1902

Armored Car, Austro-Daimler, 1903–5

Armored Car, Charron CGV, 1908

Armored Car, Bianchi, 1913

Armored Car, Erhardt-BAK, 1906

Armored Car, Rolls-Royce, 1914–15

Armored Car, Rolls-Royce, 1914–15

Armored Car, Garford, 1915–17

Armored Car, Lanchester, 1915

Tank, "Little Willie", 1915

Armored Car, Austin, 1915–17

Killen Strait prototype, 1915

Tank, St. Chamond M.16 1916-17

Tank, Mark I, 1916

Tank, Schneider M.16 CA1, 1916–17

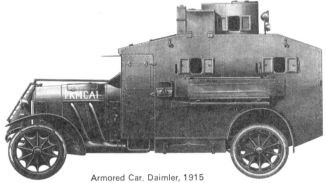

Armored Car, Daimler, 1915

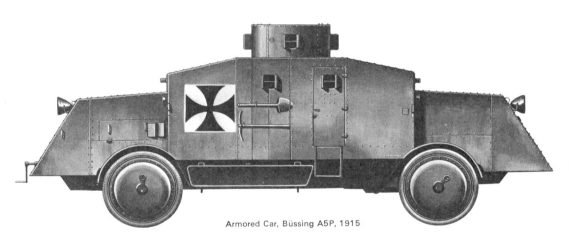

Armored Car, Büssing A5P, 1915

Tank, Renault FT17, 1918

Tank, Medium Mark A "Whippet", 1917–18

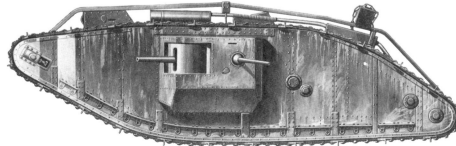

Tank, Mark IV, 1917–18

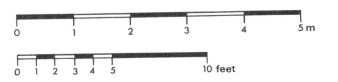

0 1 2 3 4 5 m

0 1 2 3 4 5   10 feet

Tank, A7V, 1917–18

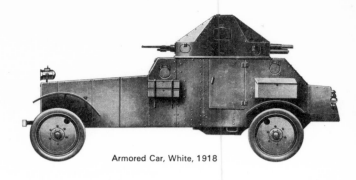

Armored Car, White, 1918

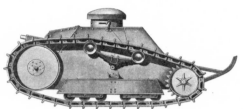

Tank, Ford M, 1918

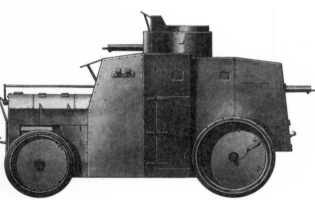

Armored Car, Daimler DZVR or DZR (Sd. Kfz. 3), 1919–20

Tank, Vickers Medium Mark II, 1923–28

Armored Car, Citroën-Kégresse M.23, 1923–28

Tank, Christie T.3, 1931

Tank, Carden Loyd Mark VI, 1928

Armored Car, Skoda P.A.2, 1923–30

Tank, B1 BIS, 1940

Tank, Renault M 1935 R, 1935–40

Tank, 3C, 1924–26

Tank, Somua S35, 1935–40

Tank, Mark VIA, 1937–39

Armored Car, Lanchester, Mark I, IA, II, and IIA, 1931

Tank, A.12 Mark IIA. "Matilda" III, 1939–42

Tank, M13/40, 1940–41

Tank, II Ausführung F (Sd. Kfz. 121), 1940–44

Tank, Klimenti Voroshilov K VIA, 1940

Tank, III Ausführung F (Sd. Kfz. 141), 1939–43

| 0 | 1 | 2 | 3 | 4 | 5 m |

| 0 | 1 2 3 4 5 | | 10 feet |

Tank, M.3 (Lee Mark I), 1941–42

Tank, A.15 Cruiser Mark VI "Crusader" II, 1941

Armored Car, Daimler Mark I, 1941

Armored Personnel Carrier, M3 Half-Track APC, 1941–45

Tank, M3A1 (Stuart III), 1942–43

Tank, T34, 1940

Tank, VI Ausführung E "Tiger" I (Sd. Kfz. 181), 1942–45

Tank, V "Panther" Ausführung G (Sd. Kfz. 171), 1943–45

Tank, IV Ausführung J (Sd. Kfz. 161), 1937–45

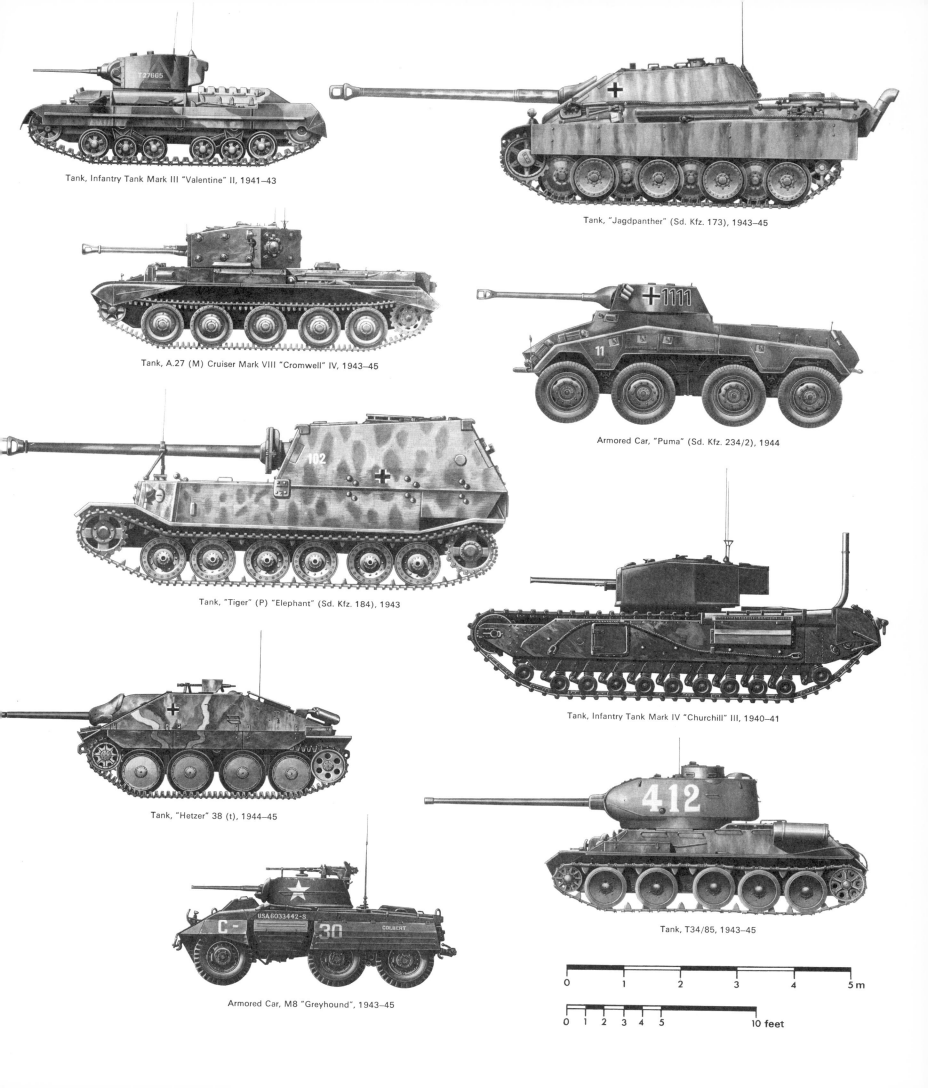

Tank, Infantry Tank Mark III "Valentine" II, 1941–43

Tank, "Jagdpanther" (Sd. Kfz. 173), 1943–45

Tank, A.27 (M) Cruiser Mark VIII "Cromwell" IV, 1943–45

Armored Car, "Puma" (Sd. Kfz. 234/2), 1944

Tank, "Tiger" (P) "Elephant" (Sd. Kfz. 184), 1943

Tank, Infantry Tank Mark IV "Churchill" III, 1940–41

Tank, "Hetzer" 38 (t), 1944–45

Armored Car, M8 "Greyhound", 1943–45

Tank, T34/85, 1943–45

0   1   2   3   4   5 m

0 1 2 3 4 5   10 feet

Assault Gun, SU 85, 1943

Tank, VI "Tiger" II "Royal Tiger" (Sd. Kfz. 182), 1944–45

Tank, M4 A3E8 (76 mm) MVSS "Sherman", 1942–45

Tank, AMX 13 Mark 51, 1954–64

Tank, (FV. 4011) "Centurion" 5, 1953

Tank, M47 "Patton", 1950

Tank, Stridsvagn Strv 103 "S", prototype, 1963

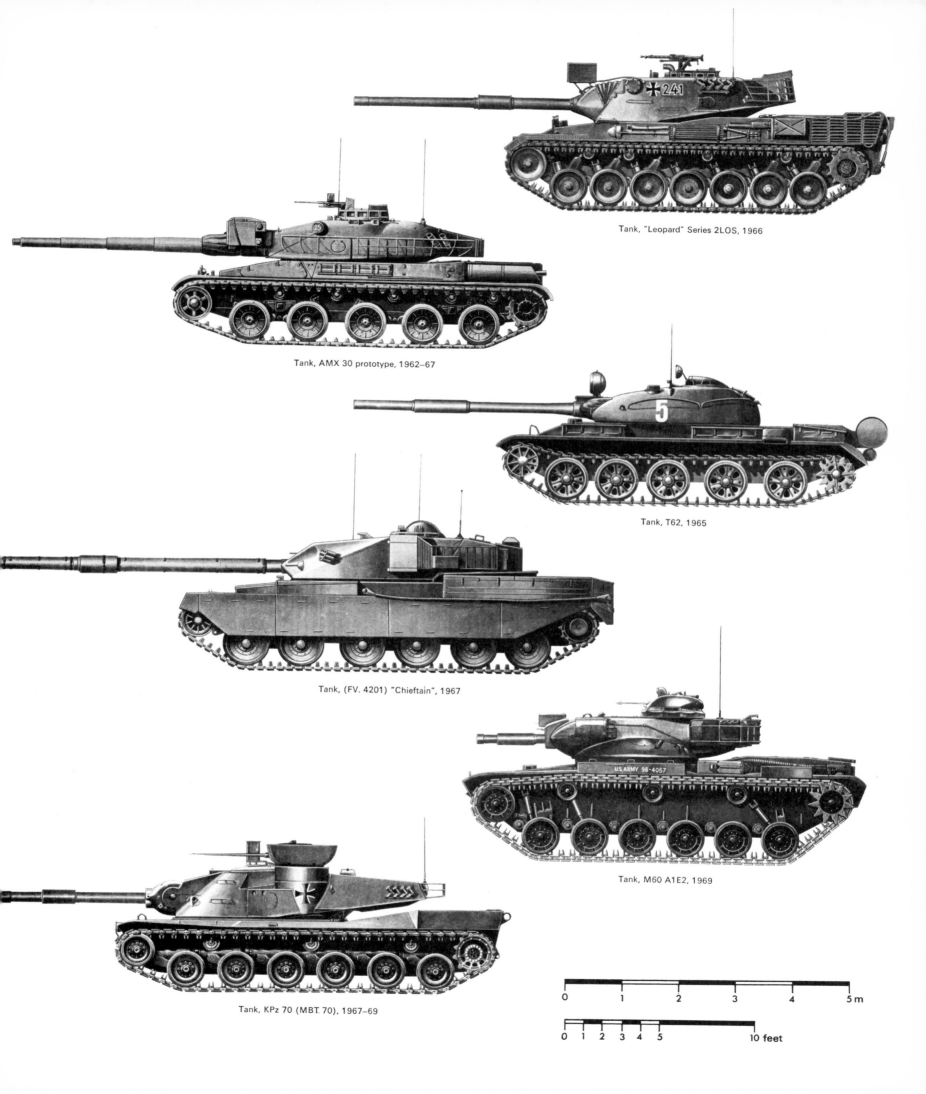

Tank, "Leopard" Series 2LOS, 1966

Tank, AMX 30 prototype, 1962–67

Tank, T62, 1965

Tank, (FV. 4201) "Chieftain", 1967

Tank, M60 A1E2, 1969

Tank, KPz 70 (MBT. 70), 1967–69

0   1   2   3   4   5 m

0 1 2 3 4 5   10 feet

WORKS CONSULTED AND FURTHER READING

ANDRONIKOW, I. & MOSTOWENKO, W. D.
Die roten Panzer. Geschichte der sowjetischen Panzertruppen 1920-1960. München, 1963.

BRYANT, ARTHUR
Triumph in the West (1943-1946). London, 1960.

LES CHARS ET LA DÉFENSE ANTICHARS
In: Bulletin de la société d'études militaires, Zürich, 1958

CHURCHILL, WINSTON
The Second World War (6 vols).
London, 1948-1954.

GÉNÉRAL DUROSOY
Saumur. Historique de l'école d'application de l'arme blindée et de la cavalerie. Paris, 1965.

EIMANNSBERGER, LUDWIG RITTER VON
Der Kampfwagenkrieg. Berlin, 1938.

FREISTETTER, FRANZ
Aus der Geschichte der sowjetischen Panzertruppe in: Österreichische Militärische Zeitschrift, Jg. 4, Wien, 1966.

FULLER, JOHN FREDERICK CHARLES
Armored Warfare. An annotated Edition of Lectures on F.S.R.III (Operations between Mechanised Forces). Harrisburg, Pa., 1955.

FULLER, JOHN FREDERICK CHARLES
Memoirs of an Unconventional Soldier.
London, 1936.

GUDERIAN, HEINZ
Achtung — Panzer! Die Entwicklung der Panzerwaffe, ihre Kampftaktik und ihre operativen Möglichkeiten. Stuttgart, 1939.

GUDERIAN, HEINZ
Panzer Leader. London, 1952.

GUDERIAN, HEINZ
Panzer — Marsch! Aus dem Nachlass des Schöpfers der deutschen Panzerwaffe bearbeitet von Oskar Munzel. München, 1956.

HUTTON, WALTER M.
Die Zukunft der Panzerwaffe, in: Übersetzungen, Folge a. Nr. 537, Kampftruppenschule I, Sprachmittlergruppe, Hammelburg, 1969.

LIDDELL HART, BASIL HENRY
Great Captains Unveiled. Edinburgh, 1927.

LIDDELL HART, BASIL HENRY
History of the First World War. London, 1970.

LIDDELL HART, BASIL HENRY
History of the Second World War. London, 1970.

LIDDELL HART, BASIL HENRY
The Tanks. The History of the Royal Tank Regiment and its predecessors Heavy Branch Machine-Gun Corps, Tank Corps and Royal Tank Corps. 1914-1945. London, 1959.

MARTIN, RALPH G.
The G I War 1941-1945. Boston, Toronto, 1967.

NEHRING, GENERAL WALTER K.
Die Geschichte der deutschen Panzerwaffe 1916-1945. Berlin, 1969.

NOVGORODOV, A.
Infantry, Artillery and Tanks — one team in battle, in: Soviet Military Review, 1, 1966.

PERRÉ, JEAN-PAUL
Batailles et combats des chars français. L'année d'apprentissage (1917). Lettre liminaire de Claude Farrère. Paris, 1937.

RADKE, HEINZ
Zur Geschichte unserer Panzerwaffe, in: Panzer, Herford, Bonn, 1959-1962, 1-3.

SENFF, HUBERTUS
Die Entwicklung der Panzerwaffe im deutschen Heer zwischen den beiden Weltkriegen.
Frankfurt, 1969.

SCHACHERMEYER, FRITZ
Streitwagen und Streitwagenbild im Alten Orient und bei den mykenischen Griechen, in: Anthropos, Revue Internationale d'Ethnologie et de Linguistique, Bd. 46.

SCHEIBERT, HORST, & WAGENER, CARL
Die deutsche Panzertruppe 1939-1945. Eine Dokumentation in Bildern.
Podzun, Bad Nauheim, 1966.

WOOLLCOMBE, ROBERT
The first tank battle. Cambrai 1917. With a foreword by Sir Basil Liddell Hart. London, 1967.

SHEPPARD, E.
Tanks in the Next War. London, 1938.

PHOTOGRAPHIC ACKNOWLEDGEMENTS

Bavaria Verlag, Munich: pages 120, 137 (below). Daimler-Benz AG, Stuttgart: page 27; Deutsche Presse-Agentur: page 154; Direction technique des armements terrestres, Saint-Cloud: page 145 (below); E.P.C.-Armées, Fort d'Ivry: pages 44, 46, 69, 71, 145 (above); Imperial War Museum, London: pages 54 (above), 54 (middle), 94; Keystone: pages 82, 124; Krauss-Maffei: pages 137 (above), 162; Magnum/Charles Harbutt: page 132; Magnum/Eric Lessing: page 116; R.A.C. Tank Museum, Bovington: pages 32, 41, 43, 49, 54 (below), 73, 89, 101; Ringier Bilderdienst AG, Zurich: page 109; American Service for Information and Cultural Relations, Paris: page 88; Ullstein-Bilderdienst, Berlin: pages 55, 56, 77, 84, 108, 125, 150–151; U.S. Army: page 158; Bildarchiv Heinrich Hoffmann, Munich: page 100.

This book was created and published by Edita S. A. in Lausanne

Lithography by Atesa S. A., Geneva

Printed by Imprenta Sevillana S.A.

Dos Hermanas (Sevilla)

Printed in Spain